GAIL G. MESPLAY

$\mathcal{A}$ MOMENT OF PEACE & QUIET

Meditations for Teachers

SMYTH&HELWYS
PUBLISHING, INCORPORATED · MACON, GEORGIA

Smyth & Helwys Publishing, Inc.
6316 Peake Road
Macon, Georgia 31210-3960
1-800-747-3016
©2002 by Smyth & Helwys Publishing
Printed in the United States of America.

Library of Congress Cataloging-in-Publication Data

Mesplay, Gail G.
    A moment of peace & quiet: meditations for teachers / Gail G. Mesplay
    p. cm.
    ISBN 978-1-57312-326-6 (pbk)
    1. Teachers—Prayer-books and devotions—English
    2. Education (Christian theology)—Meditations
    I. Title

    BV4596.T43 M47 2001
    242'.68—dc21

                                  2001018384
                                      CIP

Preface

"All our troubles in life come because we refuse to sit quietly for a while each day in our room."

—Pascal

We often start a school day in a rush of activity, forgetting to make room for the most important thing: a moment of peace and quiet. As the day goes on, we gain more and more momentum until we are traveling at what seems to be the speed of light. As classroom teachers, we need to take time to pause, take a deep breath, and think about what we want the day to be. Sometimes the chance to steal a moment doesn't occur until lunchtime or even until the last bell of the school day rings. It is vital, however, that we make some time for ourselves so that we can become the teachers we want to be. After twenty-five years of teaching I suddenly realized that if I gave myself just a few minutes of peace and quiet before school began, I could start the day focused, centered, and filled with energy.

This book is designed for that sliver of quiet time that you can call your own. There are various options for its use. You could start at the beginning of the book and work your way to the end, or open it to a random selection, or choose a topic in the index that fits a concern in your life or a mood you are feeling. Whichever option you choose, you will find a reflection for every school day and additional selections for the week before school starts and the first week of summer break. I hope you will find something on each page that will help you find a moment of peace and quiet.

In Memory of

My Father
Boyd H. Graeber
Iowa Educator
1901–1997

and

My Friend
Joyce C. Johnson
Teacher
1936–1993
Dedicated to my students,
who have given me so much.

Special thanks to:
My husband and favorite teacher, Ken, who made me persevere,
My two families for their love,
My circle of friends who support me,
Those who helped make this book possible:
Ken, Kate, Keith, Diana, Nick, Nathan, Logan, and Greg
And the many men and women whose wisdom
has been quoted in this book.

Welcome

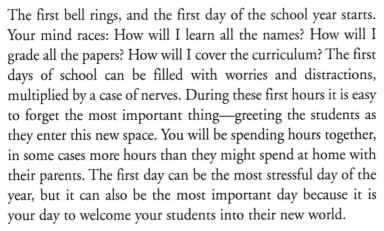

"A good beginning makes a good end."

—English Proverb

The first bell rings, and the first day of the school year starts. Your mind races: How will I learn all the names? How will I grade all the papers? How will I cover the curriculum? The first days of school can be filled with worries and distractions, multiplied by a case of nerves. During these first hours it is easy to forget the most important thing—greeting the students as they enter this new space. You will be spending hours together, in some cases more hours than they might spend at home with their parents. The first day can be the most stressful day of the year, but it can also be the most important day because it is your day to welcome your students into their new world.

"How should I live? Live welcoming all."

—Mechtild de Magsburg

1

Wishes

"Star light, star bright,
First star I see tonight;
Wish I may, wish I might,
Have the wish I wish tonight."

—Anonymous

If you could have three wishes for your classroom and the school year, what would they be? Would you wish for more patience, more desks, fewer students, a colleague to be your good friend? It is good to start a school year with some wishes, but before you make them, spend some time thinking carefully about them. Will the wishes be truly good for you and your students in the long run? Will the wishes make everyone happier? When darkness falls, go out into the night and pick one special star. Close your eyes and repeat: "Star light, star bright, first star I see tonight; wish I may, wish I might, have the wish I wish tonight."

"I wish for a smile and not ignorance, for lives of poetry, for a shooting star, for the ability to change the world, for a new muffler and memories that never fade."

—Seniors, Wheat Ridge High School

Plans

"Everything flows."

—Heraclitus

When a school year starts, we must create new plans and expectations. It would be irresponsible for us to begin a year, a month, or even a week without detailed lesson plans for our classrooms. At this time, however, it is wise to remember the advice of the Scottish poet Robert Burns, "The best laid plans of mice and men, gang aft a gley." So be enthusiastic in your planning, but always be prepared to make changes as you respond to the surprises and unplanned moments that will occur in your classroom.

"How often is happiness destroyed by preparation, foolish preparation?"

—Jane Austen

First Day, First Year

"Life can only be understood backwards, but it needs to be lived forward."

—Soren Kierkegaard

Can you remember your first day of teaching? Can you remember the space that was assigned to you and the faces of the students in your first class? You had prepared for years for that moment by taking education courses, student teaching, filling out applications, and being interviewed. You probably can recall the fear, the stress, and the joy of those first hours in your own classroom. Experienced colleagues probably tried to help, but you needed to learn on your own. We need to go back to these memories so we can remember the freshness and enthusiasm we possessed during our first days of teaching. We could find surprises in hall duty, attendance sheets, and even faculty meetings. When days become routine and "ho-hum," try to recapture the joys of your first year of teaching and bring that special freshness to the tasks that now seem so tedious.

"Anticipate the good so that you may enjoy it."

—Ethiopian Proverb

Your Place

"You must have a room or a certain hour of the day or so where you do not know what was in the paper . . . a place where you can simply experience and bring forth what you are, and what you might be."

—Joseph Campbell

It is hard to find a private place in a school building. Often our classrooms are in use when we have a free moment, the lounge is filled with colleagues, and the library is busy with students working on projects. This makes taking a quiet break almost impossible. As children, many of us had a secret place —a hidden rock, a tree we could talk to, a tiny burrow or cave where we could escape. It was a nurturing secret place that we could call home. If you had such a place, in the midst of a hectic day you can return to it in your imagination and let it bring you rest and quiet nourishment.

"What a thing it is to sit absolutely alone."

—Fr. Thomas Merton

Authenticity

"The most exhausting thing in my life is to be insincere."
—Anne Morrow Lindbergh

New teachers, and even experienced educators, struggle to define the role of a teacher. University classes outline it, school districts describe it, and then we struggle to squeeze ourselves into the job description. Unfortunately, as we try to conform into the traditional mode, we lose the beautiful core of our own uniqueness. Being real is not always easy, and we aren't always sure what parts of our authentic self are safe and appropriate to bring into the classroom. The noted psychologist Carl Rogers believes that sharing the "real" you with your students is imperative. In his book *Freedom to Learn*, he gives some advice on how this can be done: "Only slowly can we learn to be truly real. For first of all, one must be close to one's feelings, capable of being aware of them. Then one must be willing to take the risks of sharing them as they are, inside, not disguising them as judgment, or attributing them to other people."

"It is best to be yourself, imperial, plain and true."
—Robert Browning

Career

Do you remember when you decided to become a teacher? Was it in third grade when you thought how fun it would be to write on a chalkboard? Was it in college when you had to make a career choice? Was it in midlife when your job wasn't satisfying your need to help other people grow? Every teacher has arrived in the classroom by taking a different path, but the one thing we all have in common is that none of us really knew what demands teaching would make on our lives. We all thought we knew what teachers did—we had been watching them work for at least eighteen years of our lives. However, we didn't know what they did every night after school, on weekends, and even during vacations. When some teachers discover the time commitments required, they decide that teaching is not the right career. Others stay and relish how much the good outweighs the bad. How many of your students will grow up to be teachers? Do you think you have influenced this choice because of the joy you find in each school day?

Strangers

"To create a little flower is the labour of all ages."

—William Blake

They walk, run, tumble, and drag into your room on the first day of school—complete strangers. At the beginning of the year they all seem to look alike, and it feels impossible to find distinguishing features. At this point you may wonder if you will ever be able to find the uniqueness of each one. A few days pass, and you discover the one who is kind and gentle; then the next week you discover another who is wise and articulate. Each day you have one fewer stranger in your room. Some students choose to be strangers for a longer period of time. It takes more greetings and chats before they start revealing their individuality to you. Then one day you walk in and look at your class and realize that the strangers have all disappeared.

"If you break open the cherry tree
Where are the blossoms?
But in Springtime
How they bloom."

—Ikkyu

Anticipation

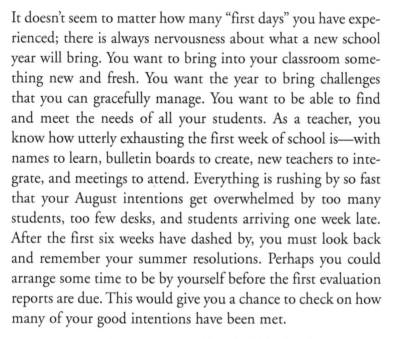

"I don't think of the misery, but of the beauty still to come."
—Anne Frank

It doesn't seem to matter how many "first days" you have experienced; there is always nervousness about what a new school year will bring. You want to bring into your classroom something new and fresh. You want the year to bring challenges that you can gracefully manage. You want to be able to find and meet the needs of all your students. As a teacher, you know how utterly exhausting the first week of school is—with names to learn, bulletin boards to create, new teachers to integrate, and meetings to attend. Everything is rushing by so fast that your August intentions get overwhelmed by too many students, too few desks, and students arriving one week late. After the first six weeks have dashed by, you must look back and remember your summer resolutions. Perhaps you could arrange some time to be by yourself before the first evaluation reports are due. This would give you a chance to check on how many of your good intentions have been met.

"Without a purpose nothing should be done."
—Marcus Aurelius

Names

""Every time we call something by its name, we make it more real, like saying the name of a friend."

—Thich Nhat Hanh

Names are important; they identify who we are to the world. We all know how irritating it is to be called by the wrong name, and we are always quick to correct the error. As teachers, an important part of the opening days of school is to learn all our students' names as quickly as possible. They feel respected when they hear that we have remembered their names; it shows that we care about their individuality. When we learn their names, they immediately become unique and special—and not just two words on a seating chart.

"Proper names are like poetry in the raw. Like poetry they are untranslatable."

—W H. Auden

Childhood

"In soft whisperings from the heart,
The child within offers you always
The thread of your truth.
May you cherish that child,
Trust that voice and weave that thread
Richly into the fabric of your days."

—Anonymous

Going back and entering a childhood memory is not only intriguing, but also a good way to reflect on what events have created the person that you are today. Relax for a moment and let your mind wander into the past; allow it to rest on one moment in your childhood. Give yourself time to explore this memory. What are your feelings, experiences, and sensations? When you have experienced them to the fullest, return slowly to this reality. Not all your childhood moments were joyous, but whatever you experienced can be a lesson on how you came to be the adult that you are today. As a teacher, you have the gift of experiencing the world with children. Remember to go back into your own childhood and retrieve some of your wonder and spaciousness so that you can share that part of yourself with your students.

"Touching childhood memories can help open us up."

—Tulku Thondup

Fossils

"An ordinary human being is a lump of matter weighing between 50 and 100 kilograms. The living matter is the same matter of which the rest of the earth, the sun, and even the most distant stars and nebulae are made."

—Julian Huxley

Fossils intrigue us because we trace the outlines of prehistoric ferns and dragonflies with our fingers and marvel at the fact that we are reaching back millions of years with one touch. Students love to say words such as "Triassic" and "Jurassic" because they ripple off the tongue in a mysterious way, just as mysterious as the image in the fossil. You ask your class, "How long ago did this insect live?" The children respond, "A long, long time ago." That's sometimes good enough, because even as adults it is almost impossible to imagine how long ago 100,000 years really was. Fossils teach us much more than just what prehistoric insects, flora, and fauna looked like. They teach us about passages and changes. When we share fossils with our students, we need also to talk about the magnitude of time and what small specks we are within earth's timeline.

"When we try to pick out anything by itself, we find it is hitched to everything else in the univesre."

—John Muir

Forgiveness

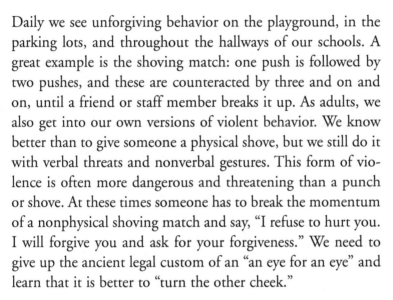

"Forgiveness is the attribute of the strong."

—Gandhi

Daily we see unforgiving behavior on the playground, in the parking lots, and throughout the hallways of our schools. A great example is the shoving match: one push is followed by two pushes, and these are counteracted by three and on and on, until a friend or staff member breaks it up. As adults, we also get into our own versions of violent behavior. We know better than to give someone a physical shove, but we still do it with verbal threats and nonverbal gestures. This form of violence is often more dangerous and threatening than a punch or shove. At these times someone has to break the momentum of a nonphysical shoving match and say, "I refuse to hurt you. I will forgive you and ask for your forgiveness." We need to give up the ancient legal custom of an "an eye for an eye" and learn that it is better to "turn the other cheek."

> *"Write the wrongs that are done to you in sand, but write the good things that happen to you on a piece of marble. Let go of all emotions such as resentment and retaliation, which diminish you, and hold onto the emotions, such as gratitude and joy, which increase you."*
>
> —Arabic Proverb
> (adapted by VanEkeren)

13

Doorway

"Teachers open the door, but you must enter by yourself."

—Chinese Proverb

You enter your building in the early morning hours. You put your key into the lock of your classroom door, hear it catch, and the door swings open. You enter a world of darkness and silence. You hurriedly turn on the lights and begin to prepare for a new school day. Tomorrow morning, if you are lucky enough to have your own room, enter the hushed, darkened room and pause. At first it will seem almost surreal—a classroom should be filled with noise and vibrant color. If you give yourself time to adjust to this quiet, dark space, you will be amazed at how pleasant and peaceful it is. Even in its stark emptiness, it is not a vacuum; the energy of yesterday is still there. Enjoy this brief time when you are alone in your own classroom with all the possibilities of a new day.

"For today and its blessings, I owe the world an attitude of gratitude."

—Anonymous

Morning

"Look to this day! For it is life, the very life of life."

—Sanscript

Salutation to the Sun

On snowy and rainy mornings it sometimes feels unfair to have to leave our comforting blankets and pillows. We yearn to stay in bed, but we do not want to have to deliver lesson plans in the early light of dawn. John Ciardi said, "The day happens with or without us." Teachers know this. We know that bells will ring, buses will deliver students, and recess will occur whether or not we are there. On most of these dark and misty days, however, we rally ourselves, struggle out of bed, and go to work because we know that our students are waiting for us and counting on us to be there. Maybe that is what makes getting up so much easier.

"Success is dependent on effort."

—Sophocles

Why?

"Know Thyself."

—Inscription on the Temple to Apollo,
Delphi, Greece

Why? This is the ultimate question. When, where, how, or whom questions seem to be ones that we can handle, or at least we can answer them with a bit of research. The why questions, however, often leave us speechless. Why did my friend die? Why do we have this stupid rule? Why am I here? As teachers, we sometimes feel we must have an answer to all the questions, but maybe our greater responsibility is to give the question gently back to the questioner. Socrates told his students that the truth resided inside them and that with work and self-examination they could answer all their own questions. He tirelessly guided them and prodded them until they found their own answers. Each of us needs to explore the why questions on our own, because the inward journey is a courageous solo trip.

"Look within . . . the secret is inside you."

—Hui-neng

Excuses

As teachers, we get tired of hearing excuses from our students about why they are late to class, why assignments aren't turned in, and why they didn't prepare for a test. Excuses are always an attempt to find an easy way out. When someone uses an excuse, it often doesn't seem like a lie to them but a comfortable way to explain why a commitment was not met or an obligation not fulfilled. It is important for us to ask our students if their excuses are the most appropriate ways to handle situations, or if honest explanations might be better. We also need to catch the excuses we make and then decide if this is the best way to handle our own problems.

"One falsehood spoils a thousand truths."

—West African saying

Autumn

"Nature is but another name for health, and the seasons are but different states of health."

—Henry David Thoreau

Do you have a special park, field, or tree that you return to each year to greet the autumn season? Some of us reside in areas where autumn arrives in such a subtle way that we must carefully watch for it. In other areas, fall comes in a splash of color and clashes of weather changes. Seasons are symbols of life's passages. Winter is a time to go inward like a hibernating bear, escaping the cold and wet for a cozy den. Spring is rebirth, young and eager, followed by the vital youthfulness and vigor of summer. Fall ends this cycle with the leaves falling and the harvesting of summer's crops. People react differently to seasons. We perform better and are happier during certain times of the year. What is your favorite time? It's fun to explore this question with students to gain a better understanding of who they are and when they will be the happiest and perform their best.

"To everything there is a season and a time to every purpose under heaven."

—Ecclesiastes 3:1

18

Evaluation

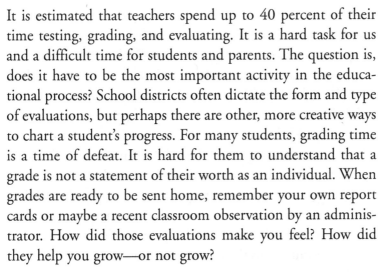

It is estimated that teachers spend up to 40 percent of their time testing, grading, and evaluating. It is a hard task for us and a difficult time for students and parents. The question is, does it have to be the most important activity in the educational process? School districts often dictate the form and type of evaluations, but perhaps there are other, more creative ways to chart a student's progress. For many students, grading time is a time of defeat. It is hard for them to understand that a grade is not a statement of their worth as an individual. When grades are ready to be sent home, remember your own report cards or maybe a recent classroom observation by an administrator. How did those evaluations make you feel? How did they help you grow—or not grow?

Addiction

"The mind stretched to a new idea never goes back to its original dimension."

—Oliver Wendell Holmes

Addicts fill up their internal empty spaces with their addictions. For a moment they might feel relief, but it will only be a temporary sensation. Filling up the bottomless pit consumes all their time and steals from them their significant relationships and a joy-filled life. William Glasser, M.D., in his book *Positive Addiction*, writes about the possibility of people having addictions that are life-sustaining, such as running and meditation. These activities bring strength and freedom into one's life. A school in Iowa has experimented with Glasser's ideas by setting aside time each day for students and staff to engage in fulfilling and nourishing activities. This, of course, means sacrificing time from the traditional school day, but it allows all members of the community to thrive in a new way.

"Positive addiction is especially valuable because it is a way in which anyone by himself can increase his strength. You can then use this strength to gain more love and more worth."

—William Glasser

Becoming

"The fatal metaphor of progress, which means leaving things behind us, has uttery obscured the idea of growth, which means leaving things inside us."

—G.K. Chesterson

Daily we watch our students changing, growing, and becoming. They, in turn, watch us. They often see our transformations before we are even aware of what is going on inside ourselves. It might be wise to sit in an imaginary chair in the back of your classroom once in awhile and observe yourself as a teacher. You might also put your favorite mentor in that imaginary chair and have that person write an evaluation of you as a changing and growing teacher. What suggestions and advice do you think this person would give you?

"Be not afraid of growing slowly, be afraid of not growing at all."

—Chinese Proverb

Sharing

"The only wealth which you will keep forever is the wealth which you have given away."

—Martial

What is the most difficult thing for you to share? Is it money, time, or perhaps material objects? Most children have a special toy they do not want to share and will grab it quickly when someone takes it from them. An adult must then remind them that they must share. They look up with tear-filled eyes and plead, "Not this one! This is the one I love the most." Because we believe that our treasures are scarce and irreplaceable, we are hesitant to share them. Think of the most generous person you know. It is amazing that, even though this person is always giving, s/he never runs out of things to share. S/he lives in a world of abundance.

"The more generous you are today, the more generosity you have tomorrow."

—Eknath Easwaran

22

Bruises

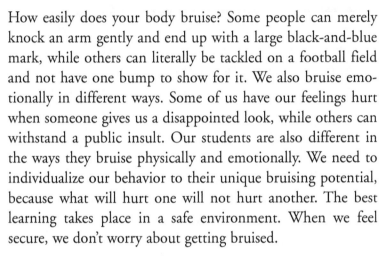

"I observe myself and so I come to know others."

—Lao Tze

How easily does your body bruise? Some people can merely knock an arm gently and end up with a large black-and-blue mark, while others can literally be tackled on a football field and not have one bump to show for it. We also bruise emotionally in different ways. Some of us have our feelings hurt when someone gives us a disappointed look, while others can withstand a public insult. Our students are also different in the ways they bruise physically and emotionally. We need to individualize our behavior to their unique bruising potential, because what will hurt one will not hurt another. The best learning takes place in a safe environment. When we feel secure, we don't worry about getting bruised.

> *"I never look at the masses as my responsibility. I look only at the individual. I can love only one person at a time. I can feel only one person at a time. Just one, one, one."*
>
> —Mother Teresa

Circles

"You have noticed that everything an Indian does is in a circle, and that is because the Power of the World always works in circles, and everything tries to be round. Our tepees were round like nest of birds, and these were always set in a circle, the nation's hoop, the nest of many nests where the Great Spirit meant for us to hatch our children."

—Black Elk

The energy of a classroom changes when all the students make a circle. It doesn't feel right if one student hangs back and makes the circle a squiggle. For some reason school architects have decided that an efficient shape for a classroom should be a rectangle or a square, so many of us fall into the habit of lining up our student desks in neat, straight rows. Students love to "circle up" because to them it seems so natural to be in the shape of the sun, a dandelion, a tree trunk, or even our planet. In many cultures throughout the world a circle means unity, and unity gives us all a feeling of wholeness.

"The world is round and the place which may seem like the end may also be the beginning."

—Ivy Baker Preist

24

Attention

"In our daily lives we may see people around us, but if we lack mindfulness, they are just phantoms, not real people, and we ourselves are also ghosts."

—Thich Nhat Hanh

How many people do you interact with in one day? For teachers, interactions with students, other staff members, and parents add up to an incredible number. We move through people so quickly that we don't have time to see their joys or needs. We all want to be attended to, and we all want to make ourselves more attending. How could you do this today?

"The power of a man's virtues should not be measured by the special efforts, but by his ordinary doing."

—Pascal

Teachers

"He who teaches a child is as if he had created it."

—The Talmud

When you have an extra five minutes, take a piece of paper and tear it into six squares. On each square write the name of a teacher who changed your life. Think of kindergarten teachers, university professors, Sunday school teachers, scout leaders—anyone who was in the role of instructor or guide. On the back of each square write a word that describes the person. Now imagine that you get to invite these teachers into your classroom for one day. In your mind, assign each of them a space in your room. Don't be intimidated; they are not here to judge you, but to enjoy you and your students. What would they love about your class? What would they be proud of? When you are done, look at the back of each piece of paper. Do the words that describe these teachers also describe you? How can you continue to learn from these mentors?

"Absolute trust in some one else is the essence of education."

—E.M. Forster

History

"Histories make men wise."

—Francis Bacon

History teachers know that one of the favorite units for students is the one that explores early people. It's unfortunate that in textbooks this topic is given the least amount of space, and there is little supplemental material on it. Students are fascinated by this period because of the mystery that surrounds these early ancestors. They left no writing to tell us about the details of their daily lives: what they had for breakfast, who they loved, who they feared, what they believed. It's fascinating to let students touch artifacts made by these people. Holding an ancient spear point or a fragment of a coiled pottery bowl allows them to connect with men and women who lived thousands of years ago. Another reason for the intrigue with these early people comes from the fact that in most cases we must dig into the earth to find their bones and possessions. This is truly a search downward toward our roots. This is also the way to uncover the mysterious parts of ourselves.

"They say the clay remembers the hands that made it."

—Byrd Baylor

Heroes

"It is the deed that matters, not the fame."

—German Proverb

If you could have a hero accompany you throughout an entire school day, who would it be? What is it about that person's presence that would make you the kind of teacher you most want to be? What does his/her personality radiate that is inspiring to you? It is probably the exact thing that you most want to share with your students. Ask your students about their heroes and how their lives are different because they have these role models.

"He who masters the gray day is a hero."

—Fyodor Dostoyevsky

Guilt

"When God wishes a man well, he gives him insight into his own faults."

—Muslim Proverb

One unfortunate thing we often learn as small children is how to fling guilt at other people. We find that guilt is a sticky substance that seems to attach better to some than to others. If you are one who easily feels guilty, you know when guilt throwers are at work. They are so good at it; pathetic face looks up and asks why you have to turn in the unexcused absence or call their parents because of missing homework. When you recognize that a student is trying to manipulate you into feeling guilty, take a hard look at what just transpired. In most cases you will see that guilt was directed at you so that a student could get his or her own way. We all need to be on "guilt alert" and also be careful that we do not use this manipulating tool against others.

"Who is wise? He who learns from everyone."

—Benjamin Franklin

Earth

"Holy Mother Earth, the trees and all nature are witnesses of your thoughts and deeds."

—Winnebago Saying

Wherever you are sitting at this moment, you are resting on about two to three square feet of planet Earth. If you could take a magical drill, bore down through the crust of this planet, and then peep down through this tiny hole, you would see a miraculous world. There would be hundreds of species of tiny creatures and priceless gems and minerals. If we think about the treasures we are resting on this very moment, we would realize what a throne we have been placed on. This planet has sustained monumental beasts such as Tyrannosaurus Rex and also the tiniest invisible creatures. It is the home to beetles, rubies, and mockingbirds. If we pause for even one second, we would realize how absolutely "in love" we are with this home. Too often we simply forget about all the gifts it gives to us each day.

"I am in love with this green earth."

—Charles Lamb

Creativity

"Imagination, what magic you possess."

—Alphonse Dauton Tartarin sur les Alpes

At birth we all receive the gift of creativity. It is a part of the human package—along with toes, a heart, eyelashes, and elbows. How sad that by the time we become adults, one of our most precious attributes has diminished, and in some cases disappeared. An even more startling fact is that in the United States most people reach their creative peak at the age of five. Creative growth should follow physical growth, with people reaching the height of their creativity in their late teens. As teachers, it is easy to see the sad relationship between starting school and the loss of creativity. Children arrive at school vibrating with bright imaginations, only to find themselves in a world where correct answers are rewarded and where they are crammed into crowded rooms where control is kept by rigid rules that force conformity. Minute by minute creativity disappears. It is imperative that we honor creativity and allow it to flourish. There will always be those who tenaciously hold on to their creativity no matter how much they are forced into a mold. As teachers, we must never allow students to lose a gift as special as their creative potential.

"The world of reality has limits; the world of imagination is boundless."

—Jean-Jacques Rousseau

Confidence

"I want to sing like birds sing. Not worrying who hears or what they think."

—Rumi

We recognize confidence in others immediately; there are people who walk into a room relaxed, glowing, and obviously comfortable with who they are. We find our own self-confidence changing according to the setting that we are in; we may have complete composure in our classroom but feel terribly inadequate when we must speak at a faculty meeting. Our self-image has been shaped by all our past experiences and by the fact that we live in a critical and competitive culture, where it is difficult to always be the "best." When we find ourselves feeling inadequate one remedy is to look at all our accomplishments. Some may seem small but tending the most abundant garden, baking the tastiest chocolate chip cookie or having the most radiant smile may be a feat that others find exceptional.

"No one can make you feel inferior without your consent."

—Eleanor Roosevelt

Friends

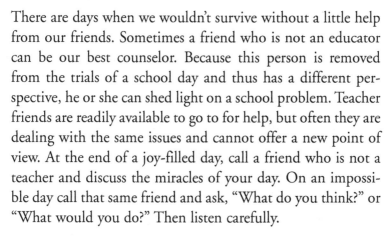

"A friend is a poem."

—Persian Proverb

There are days when we wouldn't survive without a little help from our friends. Sometimes a friend who is not an educator can be our best counselor. Because this person is removed from the trials of a school day and thus has a different perspective, he or she can shed light on a school problem. Teacher friends are readily available to go to for help, but often they are dealing with the same issues and cannot offer a new point of view. At the end of a joy-filled day, call a friend who is not a teacher and discuss the miracles of your day. On an impossible day call that same friend and ask, "What do you think?" or "What would you do?" Then listen carefully.

"There is no better mirror than a best friend."

—Cape Verde Proverb

Cheating

"I would prefer even to fail with honor than win by cheating."

—Sophocles

It's frustrating to watch our students choose to cheat, and it's revealing to ask them why they make this decision. Typical responses include: "I'm afraid of what my parents will do if I get bad grades"; "I want you to like me"; "I have no idea why I cheat." Choosing to cheat is a conscious decision, not something one does just because others are cheating. When children cheat on small things, they are likely to cheat throughout life. Research has shown that corporate executives who cheat on the golf course are more likely to cheat behind the closed doors of their executive offices. Does any one of us really want to be labeled "a cheater"? It is important to ask both our students and ourselves this question.

"We are what we repeatedly do."

—Aristotle

Gifts

"Gift giving is a celebration that unites giver and receiver. The bond is gratefulness."

—Brother David Steindl-Rast

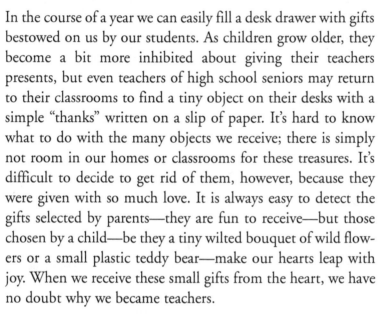

In the course of a year we can easily fill a desk drawer with gifts bestowed on us by our students. As children grow older, they become a bit more inhibited about giving their teachers presents, but even teachers of high school seniors may return to their classrooms to find a tiny object on their desks with a simple "thanks" written on a slip of paper. It's hard to know what to do with the many objects we receive; there is simply not room in our homes or classrooms for these treasures. It's difficult to decide to get rid of them, however, because they were given with so much love. It is always easy to detect the gifts selected by parents—they are fun to receive—but those chosen by a child—be they a tiny wilted bouquet of wild flowers or a small plastic teddy bear—make our hearts leap with joy. When we receive these small gifts from the heart, we have no doubt why we became teachers.

"All the beautiful sentiments in the world weigh less than a single lovely action."

—James Russell Lowell

Humble

"It matters not what you are thought to be, but what you are."
—Publius Syrus

When the Dalai Lama, the political leader of the Tibetan government in exile and the winner of a Nobel Peace Prize, describes himself, he states, "I am a simple Buddhist monk." He knows how significant he has become to the world, yet he accepts his role as one assigned to him and believes that it is no more important than any other person's task. We witness the absence of humility on a daily basis, because we all work with teachers who are arrogant and authoritarian. There are, however, always those who know how significant they are in the lives of their students and yet believe that they are "simple teachers" who are lucky enough to have been given a most special and sacred job.

"Man's character is his fate."
—Heraclitus

Joy

"One joy scatters a hundred greifs."

—Chinese Proverb

Some days are just more joy-filled than others. This joy spreads quickly, and on these days you wonder what could be better than being a teacher. Other days are not that easy, and we must work harder to recapture the energy of those bright and happy days. Sometimes this can be accomplished by simply changing the daily routine. Taking a break can often open up the classroom and create a spontaneous event that brings back joy and laughter.

"All the animals, excepting man, know that the principle business of life is to enjoy it."

—Samuel Butler

Innocence

"Little lamb who made thee?
Dost thou know who made thee?
Gave thee life, and bid thee feed
By the stream, and o'er the mead;
Gave thee clothing of delight
Softest clothing, woolly bright."

—William Blake

Wide-eyed children and newborn animals are perceived as being the innocents of the world. They seem to be incapable of judging others and appear to stand in utter amazement at the wonders of the world. When applied to adults, the word "innocent" often carries a negative connotation, as if innocent people cannot function in a competitive "dog-eat-dog" world. We often try to hide our innocence, to appear tough and ready to deal with complex and sophisticated issues and situations. Being innocent does not make us vulnerable, however; it makes us more open and accepting of others and the world.

"He is armed without who is innocent within."

—Horace

38

Clouds

"Sometimes I go about pitying myself. And all the while I am being carried across the sky."

—Ojibway saying

Are you a cloud gazer? Clouds provide a stepping-off place into the unknown. They are the veils across the boundless sky. They shelter and protect us and bring us surprises such as hail and snowflakes. Clouds play with our imaginations. While lying on our backs and gazing toward the heavens, we can create stories and then enter into them. Children remember to look at the clouds more often than adults do. Their amazement should be a reminder to us to relish the simple and to be astonished by the magical.

"Listen to the children."

—Sign on a button

Limitations

"Courage is not freedom; it is being afraid and going on."

—Anonymous

What thoughts limit you? Are they fears that you won't find love, enough money, or success? Are they concerns that you will become sick, tired, or lost? Fear, or fear of fears, limits your ability to accomplish what you desire most. It would be wonderful it we could wave a magic wand and have the fears that block our potential instantly disappear. One thing we can do when we feel blocked, anxious, or scared is to ask ourselves: Is it reasonable to be this afraid? Do we want to hang on to the feelings that limit our growth? Our students are filled with the same fears and often don't understand what is happening. As teachers, we can help them look for and label their fears as a first step in releasing them.

"He who cannot change the very fabric of his thoughts will never be able to change reality."

—Anwar Sadat

Animals

"As a child, I could not understand why I should pray for human beings only. When my mother had kissed me goodnight, I used to add a silent prayer that I had composed for all living creatures."

—Albert Schweitzer

Most people find themselves drawn to a specific wild animal. They may seek it out at the zoo, watch programs, or read articles about it. If you can identify such an animal, it might be worthwhile to examine its specific physical and personality traits. These characteristics may have great meaning for your life. Indigenous people are deeply connected to animals. Many groups believe that at one time humans and animals spoke the same language and that it was the animals who taught the people about fire and how to build homes. These people believe we all have animal helpers that are in spirit form and are always available to us. Children seem to understand this connection. They live in a world of invisible animal friends and know how much guidance the animals can give them. It's fun and worthwhile to explore this topic with our students, who often can be our guides into this magical world.

"But ask now the beasts, and they shall teach thee; and the fowls of the air, and they shall teach thee."

—Job 12:7

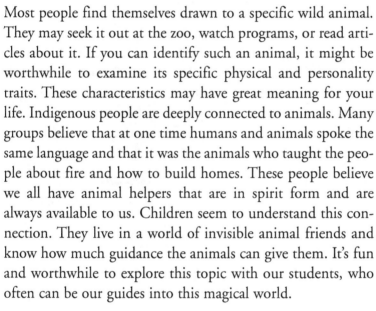

Love

"Love begets love."

—St. Teresa of Avila

There are days when our hearts vibrate because we love our jobs so much. Our students are growing before our very eyes, and we know that we are responsible for much of this blossoming. Then there are days when our hearts seem heavy and dark, and we wonder if we have enough love to keep going. Being and staying in love, whether with another human or a career, will always have major bumps and detours. Love is not easy, fast, or an end in itself. It is a daily response that we give to "the other," whether that other is a job or person. It is a statement that says I am here for you so we can grow together, even on the most difficult days.

"Tell me who you love, and I'll tell you who you are."

—African Proverb

Support

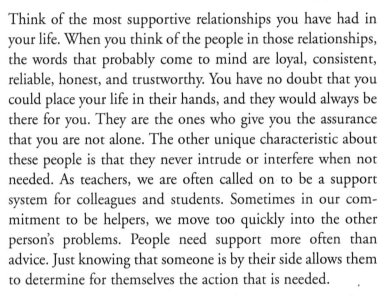

"Loyalty means nothing unless it has at its heart the absolute principle of self-sacrifice."

—Woodrow Wilson

Think of the most supportive relationships you have had in your life. When you think of the people in those relationships, the words that probably come to mind are loyal, consistent, reliable, honest, and trustworthy. You have no doubt that you could place your life in their hands, and they would always be there for you. They are the ones who give you the assurance that you are not alone. The other unique characteristic about these people is that they never intrude or interfere when not needed. As teachers, we are often called on to be a support system for colleagues and students. Sometimes in our commitment to be helpers, we move too quickly into the other person's problems. People need support more often than advice. Just knowing that someone is by their side allows them to determine for themselves the action that is needed.

"A trouble shared is a trouble halved."

—Proverb

Words

"Talking with one another is loving one another."

—Kenyan Saying

Teachers are word factories. We use words to teach, praise, control, greet, and bring laughter. Children do not have as many words and cannot use them with such agility and experience. Our words can create, but our words can also destroy. How many words do you possess in your personal vocabulary? How many of these words do you use in a school day? How often do you hear the words that you say and realize the impact they have on your students? If you could use only twenty words for the rest of your life, what would they be? You might want to ask your students this question.

"Dare to be wise, begin."

—Horace

The Universe

"I don't pretend to understand the universe."
—Thomas Carlyle

When a space mission is launched at the Kennedy Space Center, we are mesmerized as we watch a spacecraft lurch skyward in smoke and steam. It seems to be riding into the unknown on a cloud. The universe is a mystery, and though scientists can describe it, we can't seem to comprehend the meaning of such vastness. The sunlight resting on the trees outside your window left the sun eight light minutes ago and if you could travel to a star in the Milky Way and look back on your school playground, you would see children that you taught four years ago. No wonder we stare in awe at the spacecraft jetting forward; it will touch and pierce wonders beyond our imagination.

"Every moment nature starts on the longest journey, and every moment she reaches her goal."

—Goethe

What Ifs

"Taking a new step, uttering a new word is what people fear most."

—Fyodor Dostoyevsky

What if I had had different parents? What if this person had not left my life? What if I had chosen a different career? These are questions that often silently float around in our minds. They are useless, however, because we cannot change the past. There are different kinds of "what if" questions that are useful and will help us to grow. What if I took a year off and tried a different job? What if I sent my teammate flowers for no reason? What if I changed the arrangement of my classroom? How would my life be different if I asked more "what if" questions?

"Better do it than wish it done."

—Scottish Proverb

Competition

"Negative feelings toward oneself tend to be prevalent in our culture due to the low self-image people develop in early childhood, possibly because of our highly competitive society. Anyone who does not win feels that he is not good in this culture."

—Fr. Thomas Keating

Competition and individualism are two essential ingredients for the success of the American economic and political system. Thus they are values that have been taught and encouraged in our nation's schools. The difficulty with these two values, however, is that they operate on having winners and losers. We believe we must win on the sports field, in the stock market, and in all our arguments. Being a winner shows the world that we have worked hard and know our stuff. It doesn't seem to make a difference how we win—just that we win. When we have a winner, we must also have a loser, and being a loser does not motivate many of our students. As a teacher, ask yourself these questions: How can I help my students understand the dilemma that competition brings into their lives? How can I help them make wise and ethical decisions?

"Real learning comes about when the competitive spirit has ceased. The competitive spirit is merely an addictive process, which is not learning at all. This is true not only with others, but competition with ourselves as well."

—Krishnamurti

Color

"Look at that rainbow. It is only when the sky cries that you see the colors in the light."

—T'ao Shen

Do you look closely at the colors of dusk changing into night, the colors of trees reflected in a puddle, the color of the walls in your school office, the colors of your students' eyes? Do you have names for all these colors? Cultures have different ways to describe their color-filled worlds. In New Guinea the Jele people have no word for green, and the Maori of New Zealand have many words for what we simply call "red." It is curious to think that the color words in a language can shape the culture's view of the world. In 1903, a box of Crayola crayons had only eight colors; today some boxes have more than a hundred colors. Does that make our children's worldview different from our own? We all have favorite colors that make us feel bright, alert, enthusiastic, or calm. Look around your room and see how many of your favorite colors surround you. It is unlikely that the walls are your favorite color, but have you added posters, flowers, or other items with the colors that make you feel good?

"The purist and most thoughtful minds are those who love color the most."

—John Ruskin

Seasons

"Silently sitting by the window
Leaves fall and flowers bloom,
The seasons come and go.
Could there be a better life?"

—Zen Poem

Summer brings the anticipation of vacations and relaxation.
Autumn brings thoughts of starting school, rising before the
sun, fresh new faces, and papers to grade. Both of these times
are exciting and make us love being teachers, but wouldn't it
be nice to take pieces of each season and incorporate it into
the other? It would be pleasant to sleep late in the fall and see
young faces during the summer. What is your favorite season?
What is it about this season that allows you to be more fully
yourself? It is an interesting challenge to take some of your
favorite things from one season and put them into another—
for example, a Christmas present in July, sparklers for
Valentine's Day, daffodils in October. This could keep you
from getting lonely for your favorite time of year.

"But if in your thoughts you must measure time into seasons, let
each season encircle all the other seasons, and let today embrace
the past with remembrance and the future with longing."

—Kahil Gibran

Anniversaries

"Grief can be the garden of compassion. If you keep your heart open through everything, your pain can become your greatest ally in your life's search for love and wisdom."

—Rumi

Anniversaries are annual markings of significant moments in our lives. We normally think of them as times to celebrate—go out for dinner, drink a toast. But we also remember the anniversaries of tragedy and loss—the day when an accident left you with serious injuries or when someone whom you loved died. The week surrounding these anniversaries can be difficult because memories come flooding back at unplanned times—driving to school or even in the middle of a lesson. Sometimes it's difficult to control the tears when the sadness washes over us. It's almost impossible to deny or avoid these times. Even if we have forgotten the date, we often find ourselves sad and depressed around the time of the anniversary. Many of our students also experience these yearly markings of tragedy. With our help they can identify why they are sad and lonely. All of us need to honor these times by being gentle with ourselves and with others.

"Where there is doubt, faith,
Where there is despair, hope."

—Prayer of St. Francis

Sandcastles

"If you have built sandcastles in the air, your work need not be lost; that is where they should be. Now put the foundations under them."

—Henry David Thoreau

Maybe you have been lucky enough to have visited an ocean and built a sandcastle. When you construct a sandcastle you first outline the form with a stick and then start piling sand to create thick walls. Next come the turrets, towers, and drawbridges. A moat is dug, and then miniature banners are set at the four corners. Now you have two choices: leave your castle and wonder who will admire or destroy it, or simply move back five feet and wait for the tide. Slowly the ocean moves in and meets the moat, the walls collapse, and the banners are swept out to sea. In minutes many hours of labor vanish, yet every tiny bit of sand remains; it does not disappear but is transformed back into beach. It's hard to accept impermanence even if we live with it every day. Minute by minute our minds, bodies, and relationships change. When we accept the fact that change is inevitable, we will be able to live more fully in the "now."

"Life is a succession of lessons which must be lived to be understood."

—Helen Keller

Wonder

"As the sun illuminates the moon and stars, let us illuminate each other."

—Anonymous

As teachers, we see and know the power and excitement of wonder in our students' lives, and we also see it leaking slowly away as they grow older. If we compare our own degree of wonderment to that of younger children, we can see that we have much to learn from them about the enchanted and magical. They can be our guides into this world. As busy teachers in a hectic world, we aren't given much room for magic and amazement. Abraham Heschel says, "Wonder rather than doubt is the root of knowledge." As we age, we often become skeptical and cynical about the magic found in wonder. We must remember that a state of wonder is the beginning of wisdom.

"When one stops wondering at the wonderful it stops being wonderful."

—Chinese Proverb

Excellence

"Quality is not an act. It is a habit."

—Aristotle

Can you think of a time in your life when you were involved in something that you loved and were good at, that when you completed the activity you knew immediately that you had done something very well, that you had achieved excellence? An accomplished golfer once reported that out of literally hundreds of thousands of strokes he had taken he could remember only three in which he achieved "excellence." The ancient Greeks had a special word for this; they called it *arete,* and it was a lifetime quest to obtain perfection not only of the mind but also of the body. Our culture, unlike the Greeks, is not one that seeks excellence in all we do. It is hard to create the perfect hamburger in thirty seconds or the perfect house in three months. Excellence takes time, commitment, and patience. We know excellence when it occurs, for it is the moment when a collective sigh or gasp fills our classroom.

"Carefully observe what way your heart draws you and then choose that way with all your strength."

—Hassidic Saying

Pacing

"Breathless for no reason and busy doing nothing."

—Phaedrus

Teachers seem to spend a great deal of time racing around. We rush in to unlock our rooms and get materials in order for the day. We run to our mailboxes and the coffee machine. And if there is a spare minute, we rush into a friend's room to quickly wish him/her a good day. This activity gets the adrenaline going and fills us with needed energy, but the problem is that it begins to catch up with us by the end of the day. We all have different energy highs and lows, and we need to take these levels into consideration when we pace ourselves throughout our busy day. Some of us might want to slow down at least ten minutes out of every hour; others among us may find that we need time alone in a silent room. Our bodies will give us good clues about how we need to pace ourselves. Thoughtful pacing will give us a great gift—extra energy for our families and ourselves.

"Hurry, hurry has no blessing."

—African Saying

Ancestors

*"You must teach your children that the ground beneath their feet
is the ashes of our grandfathers."*

—Chief Seattle

Both children and adults love to look at photos of their ancestors. In their faces we look for our eyes, ears, and noses. We
look deeply into the pictures trying to catch a glimpse of their
stories. How we would love to know about their homes, ancestors, migrations, and transformations. It's hard for us to accept
that their wisdom might have vanished when they died.
Fortunately, bits and pieces of them stay alive in each of us. It
is important that teachers help students learn about their
ancestors so that they will know more about their own
personal life stories.

*"Never forget the importance of history. To know nothing of
what happened before you took your place in the world is to
remain a child forever."*

—Anonmyous

Neighbors

"Your neighbor is your other self dwelling behind a wall. In understanding, all walls shall fall down."

—Kahlil Gibran

In the poem "Mending Wall," Robert Frost suggests that "good fences make good neighbors." In many of our schools, paper-thin walls—not sturdy fences—are all that separate our work space from those of our neighboring teachers. And a difference in tolerance to noise can make things feel very unneighborly indeed. The noise that they are comfortable with often seems to blare into our space, or the volume of their TVs distracts our classes. These neighbors are often not easy people to have a discussion with about the noise problem. We know that it is always best to solve a problem on our own, but if this is one that's too difficult, go to the most diplomatic colleague you know; that person can probably help you work with this neighbor. We sometimes get ourselves into a puzzling maze because we fail to reach out for help.

"Do not protect yourself by a fence, but rather by a friend."

—Czech Proverb

Comfort

"Animal crackers, and cocoa to drink,
That is the finest supper, I think;
When I'm grown up and can have what I please,
I think I shall always insist upon these."

—Christopher Morley

What three things bring you the most comfort? Being comfortable is relaxation at its best; it is doing the thing that makes us feel safe and peaceful. Most often these are very simple activities that brought us secure feelings when we were small children. What better thing to do after a hair-raising day at school than to go home and do what makes us feel the happiest and safest? We never have to make excuses for these moments. They are the gifts from our past that need to be continually reintegrated back into our lives.

"If you are not good for yourself,
how can you be good for others?"

—Spanish Proverb

Aspirations

"Let me tell you this: someone in some future time will think of us."

—Sappho

As a teacher, for what would you like to be remembered? Maybe it is your creativity or your ability to explain things, or perhaps you want to be remembered for the smile you had for every student. Sometimes in the busyness of a day we forget to focus on the most significant things. We need to ask ourselves the important question: What do I want my students to remember about their teacher and the classroom we shared? Think about your favorite teacher. How would this person have wanted to be remembered? What do you think his/her primary goal was as your teacher?

"No matter what our attempts to inform, it is our ability to inpsire that will turn the tides."

—Syracuse Cultural Workers

58

This Day

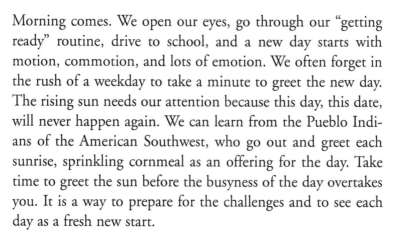

"Dawn anew sprinkles the earth with light."

—Lucretius

Morning comes. We open our eyes, go through our "getting ready" routine, drive to school, and a new day starts with motion, commotion, and lots of emotion. We often forget in the rush of a weekday to take a minute to greet the new day. The rising sun needs our attention because this day, this date, will never happen again. We can learn from the Pueblo Indians of the American Southwest, who go out and greet each sunrise, sprinkling cornmeal as an offering for the day. Take time to greet the sun before the busyness of the day overtakes you. It is a way to prepare for the challenges and to see each day as a fresh new start.

"Consider this day will never dawn again."

—Dante

Voice

"People never hear their own voices, any more than they see their own faces. There is not even a looking-glass for the voice."

—Oliver Wendell Holmes

Many people will admit that they have actually talked to a plant at some time. The amazing thing is that when scientists electronically hook up plants they actually find that plants respond in a "plant-like" way to the human voice. We must never underestimate how deeply our voice can touch another. Teachers are warned to use caution in touching their students. Perhaps we can replace a physical touch with more kind and soothing words. If a plant reacts to gentle words, think how the sound of a caring human voice must touch a student.

"O what is it that makes me tremble
so at voices?
Surely whoever speaks to me in the right
Voice, him or her I shall follow."

—Walt Whitman

Trust

"Trust men and they will be true to you, treat them greatly and they will show themselves great."

—Ralph Waldo Emerson

It usually takes days, weeks, even years for us to know someone well enough to put our trust in them. We watch to see how they deal with others and if their relationships are genuine and truthful. A few times we are lucky enough to meet someone and quickly realize that because of their openness and genuineness, they are someone who can be trusted. On the first day of school we watch our new students enter our rooms and wonder which ones are trustworthy. They, in turn, are looking at us trying to decide if this is someone they can trust with their education and well-being. Through our actions and words we need to show them immediately that we are adults who will care for and protect them.

> *"If I distrust the human being, then I just cram him with information of my own choosing, lest he go his own mistaken way. But if I trust the capacity of the human individual for developing his own potentiality, then I can provide him with many opportunities and permit him to choose his own way and his own direction in his learning."*
>
> —Carl Rogers

Worries

"If your eyes are blinded with your worries, you cannot see the beauty of the sunset."

—Krishnamurti

What are your biggest worries? You probably are dealing with home worries, school worries, and relationship worries. Every worry absorbs time and energy even when you are not conscious of the drain. Have you noticed that at the end of a relatively easy day you can go home overwhelmed and exhausted? When you have an "I can't get off the couch" evening, you might take an inventory of your unconscious activity. Sometimes just moving a worry into the conscious realm makes it less formidable. It is impossible to work on all your worries at the same time. You need to select one or two that seem appropriate to deal with and then literally take the others and put them in a safe place, close the door, and promise that you will work on them at a later time.

"Have patience with all things, but chiefly have patience with yourself."

—St. Frances de Sales

Chaos

"The unexpected often happens."

—Plato

One of a teacher's biggest fears is chaos. Nothing is more challenging than a room filled with children who appear out of control. The chaotic scene was probably caused by one student testing the teacher's limits or the spirited enthusiasm of the class clown. It takes every trick in a teacher's book to bring order back into the room, which often leaves the feeling of being drained and frustrated. Debriefing with the class after a disturbance is always a worthwhile experience. We know that this is true in our personal lives, for wisdom often comes out of some of our biggest problems and disruptions. Nietzsche wrote, "One must have chaos in one to give life to a dancing star."

"Whoever can see through all fear will be safe."

—Lao Tze

Tears

"Tears are often the telescope through which we see far into heaven."

—Henry Ward Beecher

How many bucketfuls of tears have you witnessed in your teaching career? We see tears that have been shed for many reasons: not making the cheerleading squad, not being included into a special circle of friends, not being treated with regard and respect. As adults, with the benefit of having experienced many of our own tears, we often mistakenly dismiss these young tears as "crocodile tears." Children, however, feel their tears as deeply as we do our own. We must honor their tears, as we want others to honor our disappointments and losses.

"It is such a secret place the land of tears."

—Antoine de Saint-Exupéry

Sticks and Stones

"Sticks and stones may break my bones, but words can never hurt me."

—Anonymous

We were taught this verse as children in the hopes that when a bully approached us with hurtful teasing, it would help us to ignore the taunts. Unfortunately, children learn quickly that words are as hurtful and damaging as physical abuse. Bullies exist in the adult world as frequently as they do in the world of children. They often appear smart and sophisticated, but we know who they are, and we often can't avoid their cruel behavior. Educators are told that one of the best antidotes for a student who is faced with bullies is to confront them and state that they do not approve of their behavior and then quietly and determinedly walk away. Obviously, this is not easy for children or adults. Our hearts are pumping, and fury is running through our entire bodies. At times like this it might help to think of a person in your own life who was able to meet cruel behavior head on, not with vindictive remarks, but with courage and statements of truth.

"In spite of everything I still believe people are good at heart. I can feel the sufferings of millions and yet, if I look into the heavens, I think that it will all come right."

—Anne Frank

Stars

"I wonder whether the stars are set alight in heaven so that one day each one of us may find his own again."

—Antoine de Saint Exupéry

When ancient people looked into the depths of the night sky, they believed that the stars could tell them about the future. As children, we loved to look at the moon and stars, and we believed that wishes made at this time would come true. We would explore the stories that the constellations told and were happy that night never failed to return with all its wonder. From the stars we learned about hopes, dreams, and fulfilled wishes. Tonight, go out into the darkness, and look into the sky. Find favorite childhood planets and constellations, and before you leave the darkness, find a star to call your own.

"If the stars should appear one night in a thousand years, how men would believe and adore!"

—Ralph Waldo Emerson

66

Information

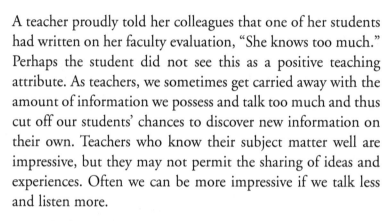

"The authority of those who profess to teach is often a positive hinderance to those who want to learn."

—Cicero

A teacher proudly told her colleagues that one of her students had written on her faculty evaluation, "She knows too much." Perhaps the student did not see this as a positive teaching attribute. As teachers, we sometimes get carried away with the amount of information we possess and talk too much and thus cut off our students' chances to discover new information on their own. Teachers who know their subject matter well are impressive, but they may not permit the sharing of ideas and experiences. Often we can be more impressive if we talk less and listen more.

"Children require guidance and sympathy far more than instruction."

—Anne Sullivan

Wisdom

"Who would ever think so much could go on in the soul of a young girl."

—Anne Frank

As teachers, we see students accumulating a vast amount of knowledge, but we are well aware that this might not bring them to a point of wisdom. Wisdom comes from experience, and thus it is a gift that often comes with aging. This, however, is not always the case. Teachers often hear profound and penetrating remarks coming from very young people. These remarks appear as if by magic and show profound insight and wisdom. We must not forget to listen and honor the wise reflections of our students.

"He who walks with the wise grows wise."

—Proverb

Time

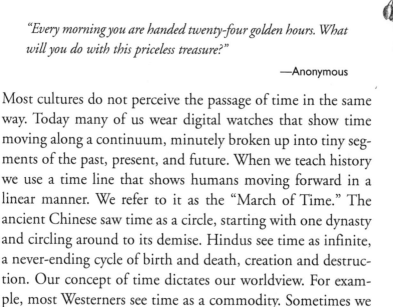

Most cultures do not perceive the passage of time in the same way. Today many of us wear digital watches that show time moving along a continuum, minutely broken up into tiny segments of the past, present, and future. When we teach history we use a time line that shows humans moving forward in a linear manner. We refer to it as the "March of Time." The ancient Chinese saw time as a circle, starting with one dynasty and circling around to its demise. Hindus see time as infinite, a never-ending cycle of birth and death, creation and destruction. Our concept of time dictates our worldview. For example, most Westerners see time as a commodity. Sometimes we have too much time, and other times we run out of time. Our classroom clocks push us and tire us; we see time as scarce and always at a premium. We must not let a created timepiece determine the manner in which we move through a day from past, to present, to future.

Pastimes

"Better to idle well than to work badly."

—Spanish Proverb

During the school year we need to take "time out." Certainly we need to take breaks during the day to be with our friends, but we also need hours on weekends when we hide our briefcases in a closet and grant ourselves hours to do what we yearn to do. This is hard for many of us because we worry about how overwhelming Monday will be. We must give ourselves time to rejuvenate by doing the things we love: riding our bike, shopping, reading, or simply puttering aimlessly around the house. The important thing is that when we do relax, we do just that! We must not let our minds wander back to grading papers or writing lesson plans. There will always be Sunday evening when we can drag out the briefcase, but we must be sure when we look inside that we do not feel guilty or overwhelmed. We must remember that we have done the most important thing for ourselves and our students. We have nurtured and refueled ourselves. After all, if we were students again, wouldn't we want our teachers to spend time relaxing so that they could come back more patient, enthusiastic, and creative?

"A good rest is half of the work."

—Yugoslav Proverb

Risks

"It is not because things are difficult that we do not dare; it is because we do not dare that they are difficult."

—Seneca

Some people find risk taking easy, while others can always find an excuse for not taking a risk—not enough time or money. Taking risks with our students makes the learning process exciting and often is the very thing that creates miracles in the classroom. What big risks have you taken in your life? What motivated you to take these risks? Do you take risks with your students? What would be some worthwhile risks for you and your students to take this year?

"The opposite of courage in our society is not cowardice, it is conformity"

—Rollo May

Birthdays

"The longer I live, the more beautiful life becomes."
—Frank Lloyd Wright

Birthdays are fun because people celebrate your life, and that doesn't happen very often in the course of a year. Birthdays are not fun if people forget them or if growing older is a burden. After our fortieth birthday, aging seems to be more and more a physical transformation: wrinkles, sags, not making the connections with the rapidity of an eighteen-year-old. These things can be alarming. The wondrous thing about getting older, however, is that as we leave youth, we are given some of the best presents of all—wisdom, self-assurance, and increased compassion and empathy. It is important that young people see adults enjoying birthdays and accepting that aging brings some special gifts. If you could reverse the aging process and actually become one year younger at each birthday, would you? Would you be willing to give up the experiences that allow you to move more gracefully through life?

> *"Even if you live to be 100, it's really a very short time. So why not spend it undergoing this process of evolution, of opening your mind and heart, connecting with your true nature—rather than getting better and better at fixing, grasping, freezing, closing down?"*
>
> —Pema Chodron

72

Serenity

"God grant me the serenity to accept the things I cannot change, the courage to change the things I can, and the wisdom to know the difference."

—Anonymous

There are moments in a day, there are days in a week, there are weeks in a month when repeating and holding on to this prayer can make a difference. Serenity can be achieved sometimes just by the act of granting yourself the time to be at peace.

"Learn to let go. That is the key to happiness."

—The Buddha

Beauty

"With beauty before me, I walk,
With beauty behind me, I walk,
With beauty below me, I walk,
With beauty above me, I walk,
With beauty all around me, I walk."

—Navajo, Night Chant

We will always have gray days. They may come because the weather has brought in clouds and mists or because we have grayness inside ourselves. On these days it is difficult to find beauty in our lives. There is, however, a simple thing we can do to prepare for such days. Consider keeping on hand things that you consider beautiful: a shell, a small art object, a framed poem or quote, a photo of a loved one. During one of these dark periods take the object and place it where you can see it throughout the school day. Let it catch your eye and tug at your heart.

"Though we travel the world over to find the beautiful, we must carry it with us or find it not."

—Ralph Waldo Emerson

Bells

"The bell invites me."

—William Shakespeare

Telephone bells, doorbells, school bells, and fire alarms all alert us and prepare us to go into action. Our modern use of bells is totally different than one hundred years ago. Church bells rang the hour of the day and told of a death. The evening bells announced the end of the day, and people left the fields and retired home for food and rest. In some meditation practices, bells remind the practitioners to return to the meditative state if their minds have wandered into the world of details and duties. In our busy world, what signals tell us to stop our work and rest? Some days it is the last school bell of the day, but in most cases this is a signal to check our calendars to see what meetings we need to attend or what appointments we must keep. What sound would be a signal for you to stop your busy workday and relax? Could it be the echo of the door clicking shut when you return home, the tea kettle whistling, or a wind chime outside in your garden? Be alert for a sound that can be your special signal so that you know when the day's work is finished, and you can enter a time that is just for you.

"The temple bell
stops ringing
but the sound keeps coming
out of the flowers."

—Basho

Simplicity

"The ability to simplify means to eliminate the unnecessary so that the necessary may speak."

—Hans Hofmann

You would think that the job of simplifying would be simple, but in actuality it is a tedious and complex task. The more we have allowed our lives and possessions to reach the point of excess, the more overwhelming is the job to simplify. To start simplifying, we need to start small. Pick just one area: your desktop, your closet, or if you are ready for the big challenge, your calendar. As you start the process, look for moments in your life that are simple moments: sitting quietly with a purring cat, slowly watering your plants, looking out your window. These moments reassure you that a simple life is attainable and rich beyond belief.

"It's a gift to be simple."

—Shaker Song

Bittersweet

"Patience is bitter but its fruit sweet."

—Jean-Jacques Rousseau

There are weeks, even months, when we look forward to arriving at school each morning. We open our doors and relish the start of a new day of learning and laughter with our students. This is a fortunate period. These days that are so brightly colored and flavored, however, can change from happy anticipation to dread. Our enthusiasm takes a dip, if not a plummet, and when late Sunday afternoon arrives, we often feel grayness settling around us. The sweetness of our jobs has turned to bitterness. If we have loved our days at school, this can be not only startling, but also depressing. During these dark times our fire seems to have been extinguished, and we simply do not know where to turn. One small thing—and at this time, all steps must be small—we can do is to take a careful inventory of our day to find what sweet moments still remain. We must give our attention to the things that nurture us; then we can regain some hope that joy will return. If the sweetness of our day can turn to bitterness, we can have confidence that the reverse can also take place.

"Great works are performed not by strength
but by perseverance."

—Samuel Johnson

Blame

"Our normal tendency is to try to blame it on another, an external factor. This tendency is to focus on one single cause, and then try to exonerate oneself from responsibility."

—The Dalai Lama

When we make mistakes that make us look foolish or inadequate, we often consciously or unconsciously blame it on someone or something else so that we do not have to accept the inappropriateness of our actions. We think, "I wouldn't have forgotten the meeting if I hadn't been given so much to do," or "I could be more patient if I didn't have so many students." As long as we place the blame on someone or something else, we will not be able to solve the problem. We need to convince ourselves that it is okay to make mistakes, because they can be corrected and life goes on. When we blame others for what we do, it is by far the worst kind of excuse.

"I praise loudly, I blame softly."

—Catherine II of Russia

Bits and Pieces

"One can only do by doing."

—French Proverb

On the way home from school do you try to weave together the "bits and pieces" of your day? Part of the review is to catch the bits that got lost in the course of a busy day and that must be worked into tomorrow's schedule. The "bits and pieces" always seem to be at the end of our to-do list, and when we start a new list, they seem to get lost in the process. We can never quite get hold of these tiny details, and that drives us crazy. We know that left undone they can grow and become enormous burdens and obstacles. Maybe we need to have a "bits and pieces" list— things that can be easily accomplished when we are too tired to accomplish the big things. We do need to take care of them, because "bits and pieces" are the little details that make our teaching go smoothly and professionally.

"Trifles make perfection, and perfection is no trifle."

—Michelangelo

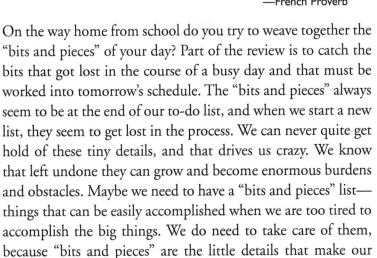

Noise

"When I got to school I ran away again in desperation for my share of solitude, without which I cannot operate as a teacher, mother, wife or lover. I'm nullified without it."

—Sylvia Ashton-Warner

"Quiet, please!" This prayer is whispered daily in many teachers' hearts. Most of the time we are noise tolerant, but there comes a moment when our whole being yearns for silence. We know how restorative it is, and how a pool of quietness can pour energy into us. Sometimes we must create a quiet space, but this is often difficult to do in our busy, churning, moving building. Another solution might be to explain to our students the healing value of silence and actually have a few moments of peace and quiet in our own classrooms.

"God is a friend of silence. Trees, flowers, grass grow in silence. See the stars, moon, and sun, how they move in silence."

—Mother Teresa

Books

"A book is like a garden carried around in the pocket."

—Chinese Proverb

If you could have only one book for the rest of your life, what would it be? If you could be a famous author, what kinds of books would you like to write: poetry, fiction, adventure, mystery? These are wonderful questions to ask your students in order to find out who they are and what books they will enjoy reading. Television, videos, and virtual reality games take children away from the written word, and unfortunately these fast-paced pastimes cannot become a friend like a book. C. S. Lewis wrote, "We read to know that we are not alone." It's a difficult task to show students that such quiet and solitary time can bring immense joy and comfort. Sometimes sharing our own love of reading and modeling this passion can be the best way to lead students to books that might become their lifelong friends.

"Everywhere I have sought rest and not found it except sitting in a corner by myself with a book."

—Thomas à Kempis

Challenges

"What is your duty? The demands of every day."

—Goethe

When we decided to become teachers, we entered a profession that is filled with many demanding challenges: explosive children, playground bullies, difficult parents. Many of these challenges call for making value-laden decisions that can cause sleepless nights and days filled with fatigue. We want to make decisions that will be good for all parties, but sometimes it's hard to get past our own self-interests. We might prefer to remove problem children from our classrooms or turn unreasonable parents over to administrators, but in most cases we know that we are the best ones to resolve the difficulties. The good thing about these challenges is the glorious feeling we experience when we have met them, gone through them, and not only survived but also met the needs of everyone involved.

"Love feels no burden, thinks nothing of trouble, attempts what is above its strength, pleads no excuse for impossibility."

—Thomas à Kempis

82

Discipline

"Perfect kindness acts without thinking of kindness."

—Lao Tze

For most teachers, discipline means not having students bouncing off the walls or talking at the same time. It means having the right amount of control so that classroom goals can be met. Sometimes we must act or react so quickly that we don't take the time to stop and determine what would be the wisest way to proceed. Remember when you were a student. Can you recall a time when a teacher, in an attempt to "get discipline," reacted in an inappropriate way and you were the target? It probably left you embarrassed or even brokenhearted. Our authority gives us a great deal of power, and we must use it with kindness and self-discipline.

"One stands perplexed and wonders whether one should use force or humble love. Always decide to use humble love. If you resolve on that once and for all, you may subdue the whole world."

—Fyodor Dostoyevsky

Boundaries

"With the help of God, I shall leap over the wall."
—Book of Common Prayer

On the first day of school in a difficult urban setting, a first-year teacher took a piece of chalk, drew a line in front of his desk, and told his students not to cross it. Some days we need protective boundaries more than others, but just because we put them up one day doesn't mean they have to stay in place. Push yourself to lower, rearrange, or remove your boundaries. Boundary lines can limit your growth and the growth of your students. When has someone else's boundaries kept you out? What kind of boundaries do you draw? What boundaries need to be readjusted?

"People are lonely because they build walls instead of bridges."
—Joseph F. Newman

Breath

"Breathing in, I calm body and mind,
Breathing out, I smile,
Dwelling in the present moment
This is the only moment."

—Thich Nhat Hanh

When tension fills our rooms, and we feel overwhelmed, one of the first things we forget to do is breathe. The brain needs fuel, and its fuel is oxygen. It simply will not run without it. So at times when clear thinking seems to fly away, one reason is that we are not breathing deeply. It's also wonderful to think about our breath when we aren't under stress. Breathe deeply when you walk outside at the end of the day, and fill up with fresh afternoon air.

> *"Sit and fill your lungs with air. With every breath you inhale a thousand billion, billion atoms. A few million billion of them are long living argon atoms that are exhaled within the second and dispersed by the wind. Time mixes them and has been mixing them for a long time. Some of them may have visited Buddha or Caesar. . . ."*
>
> —A. Rolf Edberg

Choices

"All things are changing and we are changing with them."

—Latin Proverb

What made you decide to be a teacher? How did that decision change your life? Would you make that same decision today? We all have days when we feel we may be in the wrong career. It's probably fortunate that we can't give a three-week notice; most of the time in a few days the classroom changes, and we again feel good about our career choice. At the end of the year if you still feel that you are in the wrong profession, you can investigate changing careers, or you can choose to stay in your present teaching situation and start doing things a bit differently so that you will find new excitement and challenges.

"Giving up is not giving in, nor is failing. It is no longer having to be right."

—Anonymous

Death

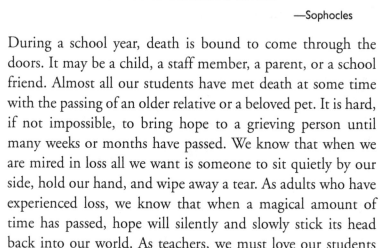

"Gentle time will heal our sorrows."

—Sophocles

During a school year, death is bound to come through the doors. It may be a child, a staff member, a parent, or a school friend. Almost all our students have met death at some time with the passing of an older relative or a beloved pet. It is hard, if not impossible, to bring hope to a grieving person until many weeks or months have passed. We know that when we are mired in loss all we want is someone to sit quietly by our side, hold our hand, and wipe away a tear. As adults who have experienced loss, we know that when a magical amount of time has passed, hope will silently and slowly stick its head back into our world. As teachers, we must love our students through their losses and help them see hope when it arrives.

"He whom we love and lose is no longer where he was before. He is now wherever we are."

—St. John Chrysostom

Myths

"The images of myths are reflections of the spiritual potentialities in every one of us. Through contemplating these, we evoke their powers in our own lives."

—Joseph Campbell

The truly timeless tales that have remained popular for well over 2,500 years are the myths of the world. We love them as much as our great-great-grandparents did, and when we read them to our students, whether in kindergarten or high school, they listen wide-eyed to the adventures of Odysseus, King Arthur, or Thor. Carl Jung, the famous Swiss psychiatrist, has explored why these stories touch the sensitive parts of our hearts and souls. He believed that all humankind shares a consciousness regardless of where or when they lived and that the myths go into this area and touch a core part of all of us. Myths have always been used to teach children the significant values of their society. They have been the most important lesson plans to teach proper behavior, courage, and valor. What is your favorite myth or mythological human or creature? These stories and characters that have fascinated and guided you would be a wonderful part of yourself to share with your students as they explore the ancient wisdom of the world.

"Stories move in circles. They don't go in straight lines. So it helps to listen in circles. There are stories inside stories and stories between stories, and finding your way through them is as easy and as hard as finding your way home."

——Deena Mezger

Quoting members of the National Jewish Theatre

Chores

"Perform every act as if it were your last."

—Marcus Aurelius

There is a romantic image of a farmer awakening at dawn, lighting a lantern, and entering his dark barn to milk his cows and feed his livestock. He is content as he does his chores. For teachers, chores are the things that we do not like to do. We all have different opinions on what these tasks are—filling out school forms, carrying out recess and hall duties, or attending mandatory meetings. We often think that we would have the perfect job if we didn't have to do "those things." Since chores are found in all jobs, we are left with only a few choices on how to deal with them: We can do them and hate it; we can do them and give ourselves a reward when they are completed; or we can do them with someone who always makes us feel good and makes any task fun. It's an interesting challenge to take your least favorite chore and brainstorm with another person how it could be made into not only a bearable, but also an enjoyable task.

"I long to accomplish a great and noble task, but it is my chief duty to accomplish small tasks as if they were great and noble."

—Helen Keller

Obligations

"Where you go, go with all your heart."

—Confucius

Many of the decisions we make every day affect not only our current lives, but also the future of many generations. Should I take the extra time to recycle? Should I form a carpool? Should I support a political candidate who will work to preserve the environment? By modeling a concern for the future, our students will see the importance of an intergenerational obligation. Our earth and everything that fills it—spiders, gems, and giraffes—all need our love and the love of our children.

> *"We have the obligation to pass on the environment intact to the next generation. We are only brief sojourners on this planet and must consider what happens after we are gone."*
>
> —Fr. Thomas Keating

Celebration

"The human heart is made for universal praise."
—Br. David Steindl-Rast

All cultures celebrate, but for different reasons and in different ways. Two of the major Celtic celebrations were held at the time of the summer and winter solstices, dates that many of us hardly notice. Some celebrations occur on the same day for different reasons. October 31 is a favorite American holiday when children dress up and go trick-or-treating. But for the ancient Celts, it was the celebration of Beltane, a sacred day when the dividing line between the real world and the supernatural world became so thin that spirits could pass through. It would be impossible to find a culture, tribe, or religion that does not set aside a time to honor a person or an event. In our schools we do not set aside time for many celebrations. We celebrate only a few special holidays that honor American heroes, or we hold a pep rally for a winning team. We do not, however, have many special days to celebrate our staff and students. Celebrations do not have to be big to be meaningful.

"I celebrate myself, and I sing myself."
—Walt Whitman

Compassion

"Until he extends his circle of compassion to include all living things, man himself will not be at peace."

—Albert Schweitzer

When we feel the doors of our hearts swing open and our concern reach out to another, we are in the world of compassion. We deeply feel their tears, and we know that if we could, we would take their burdens and place them on our own shoulders. Even if our concern cannot immediately change the event or circumstance, just the fact that we open up our hearts in this manner may help change the world by filling it with love.

"All, everything that I understand I understand because of love."

—Leo Tolstoy

Overwhelmed

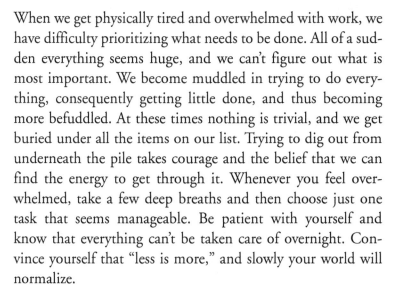

"What is without rest will not endure."

—Ovid

When we get physically tired and overwhelmed with work, we have difficulty prioritizing what needs to be done. All of a sudden everything seems huge, and we can't figure out what is most important. We become muddled in trying to do everything, consequently getting little done, and thus becoming more befuddled. At these times nothing is trivial, and we get buried under all the items on our list. Trying to dig out from underneath the pile takes courage and the belief that we can find the energy to get through it. Whenever you feel overwhelmed, take a few deep breaths and then choose just one task that seems manageable. Be patient with yourself and know that everything can't be taken care of overnight. Convince yourself that "less is more," and slowly your world will normalize.

> *"Let us spend one day as deliberately as nature, and not be thrown off the track by every nutshell and mosquito's wing that falls on the rails."*
>
> —Henry David Thoreau

Consistency

"Hold yourself to a higher standard than anyone else expects of you."

—Henry Ward Beecher

Nothing produces confusion like inconsistency. If we set rules, limits, and boundaries in our classrooms and then allow them to be broken, we leave our students in chaos. Consistency does not have to be boring or curb spontaneity. On the contrary, consistency creates a secure environment and allows creativity to flourish. We have all entered crazy classrooms where there is no visible or even invisible order. Students may seem happy in the freedom, but they cannot be satisfied with the amount of learning and growth that is taking place. When it comes to creating a secure environment, teachers are in charge. We need to accept this responsibility wholeheartedly and be vigilant, doing everything possible on an hour-by-hour basis to see that we are being consistent with all our students.

"What you do speaks so loud that I cannot hear what you say."

—Ralph Waldo Emerson

Energy

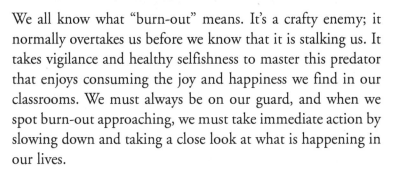

"The man is happy, we say, who knows no good that would be greater than that which he can give to himself."

—Seneca

We all know what "burn-out" means. It's a crafty enemy; it normally overtakes us before we know that it is stalking us. It takes vigilance and healthy selfishness to master this predator that enjoys consuming the joy and happiness we find in our classrooms. We must always be on our guard, and when we spot burn-out approaching, we must take immediate action by slowing down and taking a close look at what is happening in our lives.

"True life is lived when tiny changes occur."

—Leo Tolstoy

Smell

"Smells are surer than sounds to make the heart strings crack."

—Rudyard Kipling

Scientists tell us that we breathe close to 23,000 times a day. With each breath we open ourselves to odors that trigger happy and unhappy memories. Maybe that is why we are a nation obsessed with smelling good. We perfume ourselves, deodorize our homes, and read about the value of aromatherapy. What is a smell that brings you joy and refreshment? We have millions of choices: vanilla, sweet corn, lavender, coffee beans, falling snow. It's fun to explore favorite smells with students. Sampling wondrous odors often sparks hidden creativity.

"Smell is a potent wizard that transports us across thousands of miles and all the years we have lived."

—Helen Keller

Stuff

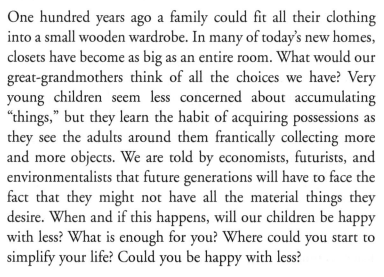

"He who knows that enough is enough will always have enough."

—Lao Tze

One hundred years ago a family could fit all their clothing into a small wooden wardrobe. In many of today's new homes, closets have become as big as an entire room. What would our great-grandmothers think of all the choices we have? Very young children seem less concerned about accumulating "things," but they learn the habit of acquiring possessions as they see the adults around them frantically collecting more and more objects. We are told by economists, futurists, and environmentalists that future generations will have to face the fact that they might not have all the material things they desire. When and if this happens, will our children be happy with less? What is enough for you? Where could you start to simplify your life? Could you be happy with less?

"What is the path from Too Much to Just Enough?"

—Sue Bender

Birds

"The blue-bird carries the sky on his back."
—Henry David Thoreau

The ancient Romans believed that by watching the formation of birds in flight they could see into the future and prophesy the outcome of significant events. To many Native Americans, birds are sacred, particularly eagles because they can fly the highest and thus can be messengers between earth and the spirits. Humans have always been bird watchers because they are enchanted with the magical ability of birds to live in the two elements of earth and air. There are many days when we cannot get the proper perspective on our problems. When faced with baffling dilemmas, we are wise to take flight and look down to see the magnitude of our problems. Examining a difficulty with a bird's eye might give us a better understanding of how to solve the problem. The flight of birds can teach us much about the scope and dimension of our lives.

"It isn't that they can't see the solution. It is that they can't see the problem."

—G.K. Chesterton

Courage

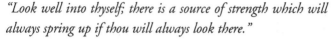

"Look well into thyself; there is a source of strength which will always spring up if thou will always look there."

—Marcus Aurelius

Courage is one attribute that we never know we have until a situation arises that tests our heroism. We can rehearse in our minds what we would do if a fire broke out at school or if we were in a natural disaster, but not until the moment is before us will we know how we will react. Discussing bravery and heroism is one way to prepare for these critical moments. Students love stories about heroes because they want to know how brave people react in a crisis. These heroes' stories prepare them for the future moments in their lives when they may be called on to act and react with courage.

"A man's courage is full of faith."

—Cicero

Fame

"Maybe one of these days I'll be able to give myself a gold star for being ordinary, and maybe one of these days I'll give myself a gold star for being extraordinary—for persisting. And maybe one day I won't need to have a star at all."

—Sue Bender

Few teachers appear on the cover of popular magazines or become celebrities who are written up in history books. We obviously do not need fame for fulfillment or we would not have chosen this profession. We do know, however, that we are tucked away in the memories and hearts of our students and that when they meet, years from now, they will talk about the moments we created for them. We will be placed in their "halls of fame." What more could we want?

"Fifty years from now it will not matter what kind of car you drove, what kind of house you lived in, how much you had in your bank account, or what your clothes looked like. But the world may be a little better because you were important in the life of a child."

—Anonymous

Darkness

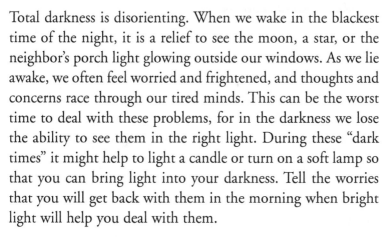

"Even a small star shines in the darkness."

—Danish Proverb

Total darkness is disorienting. When we wake in the blackest time of the night, it is a relief to see the moon, a star, or the neighbor's porch light glowing outside our windows. As we lie awake, we often feel worried and frightened, and thoughts and concerns race through our tired minds. This can be the worst time to deal with these problems, for in the darkness we lose the ability to see them in the right light. During these "dark times" it might help to light a candle or turn on a soft lamp so that you can bring light into your darkness. Tell the worries that you will get back with them in the morning when bright light will help you deal with them.

"The moment before the dawn is the darkest."

—Anonymous

Courtesy

"A tree is known by its fruit; a man by his deed. A good deed is never lost; he who sows courtesy reaps friendship, and he who plants goodness gathers love."

—St. Basil

There is a difference between manners and courtesy. Every culture teaches its young a different set of behaviors that includes rules on how to greet others, how to eat, and how to dress. Courtesy includes manners and actions that show others we respect and hold them in high regard. Courtesy takes time and concentration. It means looking into the eyes of a cashier when we thank them, not resorting to road rage when someone cuts us off on the highway, and gently correcting inappropriate behavior in the school hallways. It is taking an extra moment to ask ourselves what would be a special way to treat someone. It's asking ourselves how we would like to be treated.

"I shall pass through this world but once. If, therefore, there be any kindness I can show, or any good thing I can do, let me do it now."

—William Penn

Daydreams

"Dreams are free."

—Anonmyous

Aristophanes said that during a daydream "the mind is here, but is gone away." Erasmus said, "Though present, absent." Daily we see this phenomenon in our classrooms, as eyes glaze over and heads bob and go down. Do you remember your daydreaming moments in school? Sometimes they were the moments that got you through a day. We know that night dreams contribute to health, so the same must be true of daydreams. We all need to escape and take a brief break amid organized learning. We must honor the right of others and ourselves to take a secret daydreaming break.

"A little dreaming is dangerous; the cure for it is not to dream more, but to dream all the time."

—Marcel Proust

Responsibility

"To succeed keep on doing what it took to get started."

—Anonmyous

On many days when we depart for work we leave behind more responsibilities than we will face at school: a child with a cold, a water heater that started leaking during the night, family and financial problems. These days can be overwhelming because we move back and forth between school duties and the concerns we left behind. There is no easy solution to a life of too much to do in too little time. The only thing we can do is to keep all the concerns in perspective and prioritize in a careful and conscious way. During these periods it is difficult to be the "best teacher." But when the problems settle down at home, we can return with our old vigor to our school responsibilities.

> *"Besides the noble art of getting things done, there is the noble art of leaving things undone. The wisdom of life consists in the elimination of non-essentials."*
>
> —Lin Yutang

Humor

"Take time to laugh, it is the music of the soul."
—Nigerian Proverb

Have you noticed that there are some days when the staff lounge is filled with more laughter and smiles than others? Who knows what creates these jolly days? One joke follows another, and even the more serious staff members join the fun. Often the jokes are hilarious retellings of events in our teaching careers, the slip of the tongue in class, or an activity that totally missed the mark. The laughter changes weariness into merriment in just seconds. The joy and jokes that we share with our colleagues will carry through into our classrooms. It is so important that we take the time to be with our fellow staff members to share bits and pieces of our lives.

"If you aren't allowed to laugh in Heaven, I don't want to go."
—Martin Luther

Success

"Always bear in mind that your own resolution to success is more important than any one thing."

—Abraham Lincoln

One big goal we have as teachers is to help our students be successful—not just in our classroom, but for their entire lives. We have some good ideas about what makes a successful adult, and we try to teach our students the value of being on time, getting their work completed, and cooperating with others. We often force these values on them, however, and forget that sometimes they have to learn their own way. This is frustrating for teachers because we think we know a faster and better route to get them on the road to success. The best way to help them, however, is to stay close by, pick them up and dust them off when they fail, and encourage them to stay on the path.

"Help them to take failure, not as a measure of their worth, but as a chance for a new start."

—Book of Common Prayer

Rest

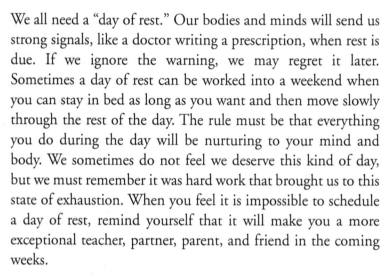

"Life is complex; we are complex. Life is simple, and the simple thing is the right thing."

—Oscar Wilde

We all need a "day of rest." Our bodies and minds will send us strong signals, like a doctor writing a prescription, when rest is due. If we ignore the warning, we may regret it later. Sometimes a day of rest can be worked into a weekend when you can stay in bed as long as you want and then move slowly through the rest of the day. The rule must be that everything you do during the day will be nurturing to your mind and body. We sometimes do not feel we deserve this kind of day, but we must remember it was hard work that brought us to this state of exhaustion. When you feel it is impossible to schedule a day of rest, remind yourself that it will make you a more exceptional teacher, partner, parent, and friend in the coming weeks.

"If you hove spent a perfectly useless afternoon in a perfectly useless manner, you have learned how to live."

—Lin Yutang

Illness

"Health is the primary duty of life."

—Oscar Wilde

Teaching is one profession where it is more difficult to stay home when you are sick than it is to go to work. It's overwhelming to wake up in the middle of the night to a sore throat or the flu and know there is no way that you can drag yourself to school. Shivering with a fever, you try to write lesson plans that a stranger can follow and that will be worthwhile for your students. It is impossible to plan ahead for those days, but we can remind ourselves that the class can survive without us. We must give ourselves permission to be sick. We might be ill because we have been so busy nurturing others that we forgot to take care of ourselves. In the dark dawn of one of these mornings quickly write out your plans, go back to bed, and try hard not to think about your class for at least twelve hours.

"Ultimately, we will be healthier, not because of new drugs or surgical techniques but because of the things we do for ourselves."

—Louis Sullivan

Astonishment

"The wise man is astonished by everything."

—Andre Gide

Astonishment ("God-filled") sweeps us into another realm, leaving us speechless because the moment defies words. Moments of astonishment most often come as surprises: the harvest moon peaking into our windows, the grin of understanding flashing across the faces of children. These moments are some of the greatest gifts that life bestows. We must be careful never to close ourselves off from these moments, because to be a receiver we must be ready to stand in astonishment.

"Come here! There are little animals in this water. Look! See what I have discovered."

—Antoine Van Leeuwenhoek

Homework

"To do nothing is sometimes a great remedy."

—Hippocrates

When students complain about their many assignments, it's hard for them to believe that teachers have as much homework as they do. We take home papers to grade, lesson plans to write, committee reports, and work from college classes. Teaching would be an almost perfect job if we didn't have so much homework! Just as an experiment, one night refuse to take home any work so that you will have time to relax for a few hours. You will probably sleep better and return to work feeling like you have had a vacation. Our students also need breaks once in awhile from their homework. When they return from their mini-vacation, they will be refreshed and very grateful for the teacher who understood that everyone needs some time off.

"Every now and then go away, have a little relaxation, for when you come back to your work your judgement will be better. Go some distance away because then the work appears smaller and more of it can be taken in at a glance and proportion is readily seen."

—Leonardo da Vinci

Promises

"He who is most slow in making a promise is the most faithful in the performance of it."

—Jean-Jacques Rousseau

Daily we make promises: "I promise to be more organized"; "I promise to be more punctual"; "I promise to be more patient." When we break big promises, we feel heartbroken and unworthy because we know that it has hurt our credibility. Being given a promise makes one feel honored and special, and if that promise is broken, we often lose trust and admiration for the promise maker. Children will learn the value and importance of promises only if we keep our promises to them. If we break our promises, they will grow to understand that promises are arbitrary things. Sometimes a promise has to be broken, but then it is imperative that we give a clear and truthful explanation of why it could not be fulfilled. "Promises are promises."

"A mind that is conscious of its integrity scorns to say more than it means to perform."

—Robert Burns

Questions

"A correct answer is like an affectionate kiss."

—Goethe

As teachers, we ask questions all day long. Some are questions that have easy and fast answers, but many require time for students to find creative solutions. The more open-ended the question, the more time is needed for a response. We find answers to puzzling questions at unexpected times and in unexpected places: taking a walk, playing sports, or standing in a hot shower. Often the best answers come when we are thinking about a totally different subject or even when we're daydreaming. It's important to remember to give our students the time to come up with answers in their own way. What questions do you continually ask yourself? Where do you go to find answers to these questions? Where is your best thinking spot?

"When a question is posed, ceremoniously the universe responds."

—Chinese Proverb

Diversity

"I do not want my house to be walled in on all sides and my windows to be stuffed. I want the cultures of all lands to be blown about my house as freely as possible."

—Gandhi

As children grow, they struggle to define who they are as people. They study their world and observe, "I am like this person, and I am not like that person." They sort and sift and slowly define their uniqueness. "I am black, I am female, I am poor, I am smart, etc." This is a necessary process for all of us, but the danger is that by discovering who we are like, we sometimes begin to think that those who are different are less important or valuable. Defining ourselves rigidly can make our world an exclusive one. If we live in a world that does not find wisdom and joy in diversity, our lives will be colorless and boring. If all trees were junipers, and if our only food were soup, we would soon lose our curiosity to explore the world. As teachers, we realize that one of our greatest responsibilities is to open our students' eyes to accepting the world of differences so that they can enjoy the richness of diversity.

"Children know in their minds that all children are the same, all human beings are the same."

—The Dalai Lama

Elders

"Those who do not listen to the voice of the elderly are like trees without roots."

—Bayaka Proverb

Our society is often prejudiced against the elderly, who are isolated from the mainstream of daily activity in retirement homes and nursing centers. In a culture that values youth, strength, and vitality over quiet wisdom, some believe the elderly are not making significant contributions. In other cultures the elderly are seen as the pillars of the society, dispensing wisdom and keeping order through their insight and advice. Life is a series of passages from infancy to youth, to young adulthood, to middle age, to old age. All stages have much to share with the others, and we have an obligation to show our students the value of each passage and the beauty of aging.

"The moral progress of mankind is due to the aged. The old grow better and wiser."

—Leo Tolstoy

Satisfaction

"If you have inner peace, the external problems do not affect your deep sense of tranquility. You are happy regardless of circumstances."

—The Dalai Lama

Concluding a school day is a lot like finishing a meal—you know immediately whether or not you feel satisfied. When the day is over and we close and lock our door, we know immediately whether we feel full or empty. If there is an empty feeling, it may come from knowing a lesson wasn't completed or a phone call to a parent wasn't made. But more likely it is from the fact that we didn't connect with a child through a wink or a smile, or we did not have the patience with the class that we had resolved to deal with more gracefully and consciously. Then there are days when we leave school feeling wondrously full. Everything was done just as we had planned: lessons completed, papers graded, happy students. On the days that we feel a certain amount of emptiness in the pit of our stomachs we must look back on the exceptional days and know that they will return.

"You can tell how good a deed was by how big a thrill you got out of doing it."

—Anonymous

Emergency

"They only survive who stand and wait."

—John Milton

It seems that an emergency room demands the most patience in the world. A crisis occurs, and you anxiously race to the hospital. And then you wait. You wait to check in, you wait for a room, and you wait for a nurse, the doctor, an X-ray. Throughout this time you believe that everyone should be rushing around taking care of your situation, but instead everyone seems to be moving in slow motion. Nurses and doctors quietly appear and disappear, and you want to yell at them to come to your cubicle and take care of your situation. Perhaps there is a lesson here: In moments requiring quick and urgent action, you need to catch your breath and move slowly. Emergencies are truly the time to practice patience.

"You gain strength, courage, and confidence by every experience in which you really stop to look fear in the face. You must do the thing you cannot do."

—Eleanor Roosevelt

Food

All religions, cultures, and communities celebrate their shared lives and beliefs by eating together. It would be very strange, indeed, to celebrate any special occasion without food. We look forward to the church potluck, faculty picnic, and family Thanksgiving feast. Planning, preparing, and serving a meal to those we love is one of the most exquisite gifts we can give. These special feasts are truly the opposite of the scene in a school cafeteria where food is anxiously awaited with much pushing and shoving in line. Lunch is eaten quickly in order to get back to class, and students leave garbage on the tables and floors for the custodians to clean. Our fast food and fast lifestyle are present in our school lunchrooms. In most homes, meals are no longer a time when families are able to share slowly and peacefully their days and their thoughts. There doesn't seem to be time in our busy lives to savor every bite of food with thoughts of the many people who made the moment possible.

Gossip

"We would have much peace if we would not busy ourselves with the sayings and doings of others."

—Thomas à Kempis

We have all heard conversations change gradually from an enlightening exchange to simple gossip. The latter does not take much energy or thought, and it also brings a certain excitement. Surely some gossip is harmless, but it can also be hurtful and damaging. Often the person sharing the gossip is telling the truth about a situation, but the parts that are overly embellished or omitted can cause confusion or harm. The other problem with gossip is that in the retelling of a story, facts become increasingly distorted. When we hear harmful gossip, we can stop the momentum by gently steering the topic to something new or by making corrections. If these maneuvers do not work, we can simply walk away. Hopefully if we refuse to join in, others will also understand the harm or hurt that is being done. Gossip is often at the expense of another, and we need to be careful not to cause someone pain by being a part of this kind of conversation.

"Who brings a tale takes two away."

—Irish Proverb

Habits

"Habit is habit and cannot be flung out a window by man, but coaxed downstairs a step at a time."

—Mark Twain

We are all creatures of habit; if we weren't, it would take us a long time to get out of the house every morning. The more we repeat a specific action, the more automatic it becomes and thus the more accurately it is imprinted on the brain. It would be a nuisance to go around having to think how to brush our teeth or how to drive to school each morning. Habits keep us moving in the right direction. Obviously there is a downside to this: once habits are imprinted, they are hard to erase. We all have a few habits that, if eliminated, would make us happier and more spontaneous individuals. As an experiment, during one day catch the habits that you find irritating. Try not to make excuses, but with a bit of patience, slowly, day by day, catch and release them.

"Habit is overcome by habit."

—Erasmus

Juggler

"It's not enough to be busy . . . the question is, what are we busy about?"

—Henry David Thoreau

Teachers are experienced jugglers. By the time we drive into the parking lot, we are juggling at least three things. When we open our classroom door, two more balls go up, and by the time we check our mailboxes, three more balls have taken flight. The count is now eight, an amazing feat even for professional entertainers. When we watch experienced jugglers, they appear to be perpetual-motion machines, and the only way they can bring the movement to a halt is by handing the balls, one by one, to a partner or by carefully placing each one on a stationary object. There are many days when we feel that we are in perpetual motion, and we don't know how to stop the momentum. At times like this we need to learn from the professionals and pass some of the balls to a partner or just place them in a basket, take a bow, and walk away.

"One never notices what has been done; one can only see what yet remains to be done."

—Marie Curie

Hands

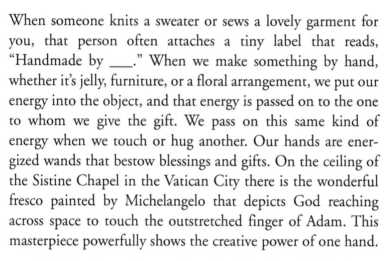

"Flowers leave some of their fragrance in the hand that bestows them."

—Chinese Proverb

When someone knits a sweater or sews a lovely garment for you, that person often attaches a tiny label that reads, "Handmade by ___." When we make something by hand, whether it's jelly, furniture, or a floral arrangement, we put our energy into the object, and that energy is passed on to the one to whom we give the gift. We pass on this same kind of energy when we touch or hug another. Our hands are energized wands that bestow blessings and gifts. On the ceiling of the Sistine Chapel in the Vatican City there is the wonderful fresco painted by Michelangelo that depicts God reaching across space to touch the outstretched finger of Adam. This masterpiece powerfully shows the creative power of one hand.

"God alone knows the secret plan of the things He will do for the world using my hand."

—Toyohiko Kagawa

Growth

On a daily basis we see our students changing physically. We see them growing taller, and we hear their voices changing. Inner growth, however, is not as obvious. It often occurs in spurts, sometimes stopping abruptly or being blocked momentarily by events beyond an individual's control. Both physical and internal growth take patience and willpower; sometimes the changes can overwhelm us. How can we help our students understand the nature of growth and transformation so that they, too, can learn patience?

Heart

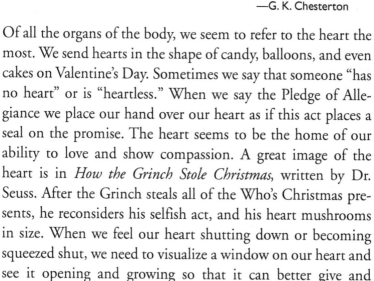

Of all the organs of the body, we seem to refer to the heart the most. We send hearts in the shape of candy, balloons, and even cakes on Valentine's Day. Sometimes we say that someone "has no heart" or is "heartless." When we say the Pledge of Allegiance we place our hand over our heart as if this act places a seal on the promise. The heart seems to be the home of our ability to love and show compassion. A great image of the heart is in *How the Grinch Stole Christmas*, written by Dr. Seuss. After the Grinch steals all of the Who's Christmas presents, he reconsiders his selfish act, and his heart mushrooms in size. When we feel our heart shutting down or becoming squeezed shut, we need to visualize a window on our heart and see it opening and growing so that it can better give and receive love.

Honesty

"Where is there dignity without honesty?"

—Cicero

When we teach our students about the value of honesty, we often use the examples of two American boys: George Washington and Abraham Lincoln. Young George went into his mother's carefully tended garden and hacked down her favorite tree. Instead of blaming it on another, he bravely admitted: "I cannot tell a lie; I chopped down the cherry tree." As a teenager, Lincoln accidentally overcharged a customer at the general store where he worked and then walked many miles to return just a few pennies. Regardless of their historical accuracy, these two stories about men who grew up to be politicians have entered American mythology. Students do not know many adults who would go to their bosses and confess a dishonest act or who believe it is important to be honest about even the smallest things. They see little in the newspapers that leads them to believe that our nation's leaders follow in the footsteps of Washington and Lincoln. Students will learn about the value of honesty by watching the adults they admire. Do your actions and words show your students that you are an honest person?

"It does not require many words to speak the truth."

—Chief Joseph, Nez Perce

Trees

"He who plants a tree loves others besides himself."

—English Proverb

Some of us have a favorite tree that we consider a friend. It may be one that we shared secrets with as a child or one that we planted to commemorate a special event. Trees have the ability to reach out to us and give us joy, comfort, and strength. Can you imagine a world without trees? If you remove the trees, you remove the birds. If you remove the birds, you remove the most beautiful morning songs. And if you allow the trees of the rainforests to be removed, indigenous people will lose the land that has been their homes for many centuries. We cannot afford to betray the trees of the world that have made our planet both habitable and wondrous. If you are fortunate enough to have a tree growing outside your classroom window, it's a beautiful and healthy distraction for you and your students. This tree may be a wonderful way to begin to explore the friendship that trees and humans have always enjoyed.

> *"Every day look at a tree. As you approach it, practice breathing in and out, and when you get there, hug the tree . . . and smell its bark, so fragrant. If you do that, in a few weeks you will feel much better."*
>
> —Thich Nhat Hanh

Hoops

"Whatever you do may seem insignificant, but it is most important that you do it."

—Gandhi

One of the reasons we love to go to the circus is that so many of the acts are metaphors for our lives. There are days when we walk a tightrope or jump like the wonderfully trained animals through hoops. In our lives, hoops are generally the duties and tasks that don't seem to have much use or significance. Good hoop-jumpers get rewarded with applause and prizes, but often they aren't the ones who make significant contributions. Hoop-jumping can be stressful because we have more important things to do in a busy school day. It's hard to convince hoop-creators that a few could be taken out of the act, but until that happens we must jump as quickly as we can and run off the stage so that we can get down to the real work.

"Never give up. Never give up. Never, never, never. Never, in anything great or small, large or petty, never give in except to convictions of humor and good sense."

—Winston Churchill

126

Quietness

"I named this place Listening Point because only when one comes to listen, only when one is aware and still, can things be seen and heard. Everyone has a listening point somewhere. It does not have to be in the north or close to the wilderness, but some place of quiet where the universe can be contemplated in awe."

—Sigurd Olson

We all must have a quiet place, a place that restores us and lets us practice the art of listening. Where do you go to listen to the soft and easy sounds that prepare you for the times that are filled with chaotic noise? We can practice the art of listening by concentrating and focusing on soft and quiet sounds: soothing music, a gentle brook, or a purring cat. These moments will teach us how to listen more carefully to students when they need someone to hear their thoughts and problems. Is there a way for you to create a "listening point" or a listening time before you start or end your day?

"Nature seems to have provided us with the need for silence. We seek it as we seek returning to a place of security, warmth and love."

—Fr. Thomas Merton

Rebellion

"To err is human."

—Alexander Pope

We become rebellious when we are overwhelmed and have little control over the events in our lives. Students get overwhelmed with too much homework and too many tests and often refuse to do them. Teachers also get overwhelmed because they are expected not only to write lesson plans and grade papers, but also to be a part of many school activities. When our days are too full, we often rebel by not finishing certain tasks or not showing up for meetings. When rebellious behavior takes place, it is important to stop and take a careful look at what is happening. When you see students becoming restless, take a look at what you are asking them to do. Hopefully when you and your colleagues feel this same restlessness your administration will also be willing to listen to your needs.

"A little rebellion now and then is a good thing."

—Thomas Jefferson

Laughter

"One joy dispels a thousand cares."

—Chinese Proverb

Laughter is joy that overflows. A room can ring with laughter, and the energy that comes from a joy-filled experience can make a day a blessing. Have you noticed that there are some teachers who never laugh in their classrooms? Perhaps they fear that if their students see them giggling with joy, they will appear more human and thus lose the tight control they feel they need. Do you allow your students to make you laugh? What makes your classroom erupt in laughter? How many times did your class laugh freely and together this week?

"Those who bring sunshine to the lives of others can not keep it from themselves."

—Anonmyous

Transformation

"Everything changes, nothing remains without change."

—The Buddha

We are told that a snake in the process of shedding its skin is overly sensitive and agitated. This is not hard to believe because anyone who is forced to change is bound to feel powerless, frightened, and insecure. Sometimes we choose to enter into moments of transformation, and other times the moments are chosen for us. Like the snake that has no choice, we need to accept the change with all its insecurities and know that we have been given the great gift of transformation.

"Remember what you have seen, because what is forgotten returns to the wind."

—Navajo Chant

Leadership

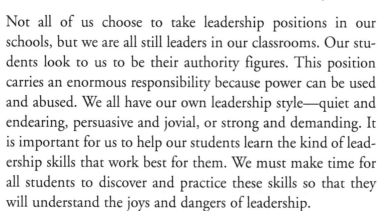

"Don't command, convince."

—Anonymous

Not all of us choose to take leadership positions in our schools, but we are all still leaders in our classrooms. Our students look to us to be their authority figures. This position carries an enormous responsibility because power can be used and abused. We all have our own leadership style—quiet and endearing, persuasive and jovial, or strong and demanding. It is important for us to help our students learn the kind of leadership skills that work best for them. We must make time for all students to discover and practice these skills so that they will understand the joys and dangers of leadership.

"A good heart and a good mind—those are what you need to be a chief."

—Louis Farmer, Onondaga Chief

Regrets

"To regret deeply is to live afresh."

—Henry David Thoreau

At the end of a day, week, or semester we always have a few regrets about the things we neglected or did not complete. It is wise to stop periodically and evaluate our lives because this is the only way we will be able to improve our teaching. Spending too much time, however, can turn our regrets into guilt, and even guilt about feeling guilty. The tug of regret can only be worthwhile if we evaluate its sources and let it take us to a new place. Regrets should lead to change in a positive way.

"Never look back unless you are planning on going forward."

—Anonmyous

Fools

"He deserves Paradise who makes his companions laugh."
—The Koran

"Don't be foolish." "Act your age." "What will people think?" When we break out of the way things are normally done, people often attempt to bring us back into the box of acceptable behavior. When they can't make us conform, they throw up their hands and say, "She just marches to the beat of a different drummer." All societies have norms that govern behavior; these are necessary, but they can also bring about a stagnant environment. Many cultures realize this; so they allow a few fools. In medieval culture there was the jester; in the American Southwest, Native Americans have the Kosheres, or clowns who make fun of members of their own community and of the tourists who attend the ceremonials. These characters push people to look at themselves and laugh at their own foolish ways. Every classroom has a few clowns and jokers who can be annoying and disruptive, but they also might be the ones who are able to bring a different perspective on what is taking place in our learning environment.

"Don't postpone joy."
—Slogan on a button

Learning

"Learning is movement from moment ot moment."

—Krishnamurti

As teachers, we know that there are as many ways to learn as there are students in our classrooms. We sometimes forget this and think that the way we learn is the same way that others learn. When time is at a premium, it is often convenient to try to get everyone moving along the same learning path. This approach will only lead to frustrated students who will quickly tune out or become disruptive. It is imperative that we be aware of the different ways people take in knowledge and honor each student's unique style.

"Some people will never learn anything because they understand everything too soon."

—Alexander Pope

Resentment

"The remedy for wrongs is to forget them."

—Publius Syrus

One of the hardest things for us to say is, "I forgive you." Sometimes the act that needs forgiveness is as small as a thoughtless driver cutting us off on the way to school or a student who distracts us in the middle of an activity. If we don't say, "I forgive you," the disappointment and anger will take up a permanent residence inside us, and more resentment will move in. Being able to forgive will help our hearts open and clear out old resentments, thus allowing us to be more patient and loving people.

"The weak can never forgive. Forgiveness is an attribute of the strong."

—Gandhi

Hope

"My hopes are not always realized but I hope."

—Ovid

When we hope for something, we are projecting our wishes into the future: I hope for a smaller class this year; I hope for a raise; I hope for a new teaching assignment. When we believe that these are all possibilities, it is amazing how many do come true. Patience is a necessary ingredient of hope because sometimes our timeframe is not the same one that the universe has in mind. Make your hopes wise and optimistic— and of course it is always permissible to cross your fingers. What in your life gives you hope? Where do you need to be more patient?

"Most people look at what is and never see what can be."

—Albert Einstein

Exhaustion

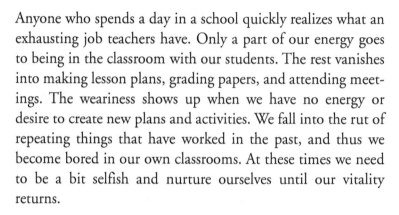

"Life is so short we must move very slowly."

—Thai Proverb

Anyone who spends a day in a school quickly realizes what an exhausting job teachers have. Only a part of our energy goes to being in the classroom with our students. The rest vanishes into making lesson plans, grading papers, and attending meetings. The weariness shows up when we have no energy or desire to create new plans and activities. We fall into the rut of repeating things that have worked in the past, and thus we become bored in our own classrooms. At these times we need to be a bit selfish and nurture ourselves until our vitality returns.

"We cannot do all things."

—Virgil

137

Humility

"The higher we are placed, the more humble we should walk."

—Cicero

It's easy to spot humble people. They contain an inner radiance and seem to be unaware of their uniqueness. Mother Teresa is a good example. She was loved and honored throughout the world, yet showed no trace of arrogance or pride. We love gentle and humble people, but sometimes we see them as being sweet and naive, rather than the moral giants of our world. Our students often idolize rock and film stars who do not display humility but try to be bigger than life with artificial flash and showmanship. Humility comes when we accept our talents as marvelous gifts that need to be generously shared with others.

"A truly great man never puts away the simplicity of a child."

—Chinese Proverb

Listening

"Nature gave us one tongue and two ears so we could hear twice as much."

—Epictetus

As teachers, we realize that one of our most important skills and duties is be a master listener. Sometimes, however, there is so much noise that it is hard to hear the most important things. Perhaps we need training in selective hearing so that we can tune out the sounds that interfere with what we truly need to hear. When we are listening to someone, it must be a full-time task; we must not be thinking or doing anything else. If we model attentive listening, our students will learn to do the same with others. This may be one of the most important things we can teach them.

"The most difficult thing of all is to keep quiet and listen."

—Aulus Gellius

Impossibilities

"Even if I knew that tomorrow would go to pieces, I would still plant my apple tree."

—Martin Luther

"This schedule . . . this student . . . this teammate . . . this room . . . is impossible." Does this sound familiar? Our students also live in a world filled with impossibilities: impossible parents, impossible neighborhoods, and impossible diets. Being young, they have little or no control over most of these conditions, nor do they know that their lives will not always be this way. Because they do not have the benefit of our years of experience, they may not understand that things do change and that they must always be hopeful. As adults, we need to give them confidence that impossibilities can turn into possibilities.

"Man is harder than rocks and more fragile than an egg."

—Yugoslav Proverb

Expectations

"... everything, absolutely everything counts."

—Sogyal Rinpoche

We hear the word "expectations" often in the teaching profession. We are told to state our expectations clearly at the beginning of the year so that our students will not have to spend time trying to figure out what is appropriate behavior in our classrooms. We also hear about the research that shows what teachers expect from their students is what they do. For example, in classrooms where teachers expected the girls to be better readers than the boys, that is exactly what occurred. This is significant information. It means that the thoughts we have can actually be manifested in our room. It is important for us to examine our expectations constantly so that they are accurate and allow us to treat all our students in a just and fair manner.

"Human beings, by changing the inner attitudes of their minds, can change the outer aspects of their lives."

—William James

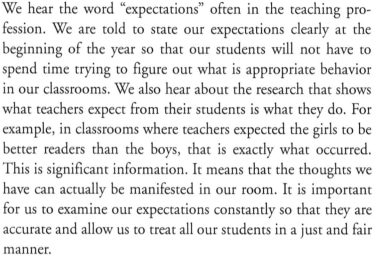

Intuition

"A moment's insight is sometimes worth a life's experience."
—Oliver Wendell Holmes

Intuition comes from the Latin word *tueor,* which means to gaze, contemplate, protect. We are all born with the gift of intuition, but most of us have lost it bit by bit as we try to survive in a culture that puts greater value on reason and logic. Intuition speaks in many ways; sometimes it is just a tiny whisper in our ear, and other times it might come as a big hunch with thunderous reverberation in our head. When we see someone silently, thoughtfully cock their head, they might be listening to this voice. We must encourage and allow room for these unseen counselors to give wise advice to our students.

"The intellect has little to do on the road to discovery. There comes a leap of consciousness, call it intuition or what you will, and the solution comes to you and you don't know how or why."
—Albert Einstein

Patience

"Patience is needed with everyone, but first of all with ourselves."

—St. Frances de Sales

Have you noticed that there are days when you have ten times more patience than other days? Maybe it was caused by a good night's sleep, the encouraging note you found in your mailbox, or the fact that you were able to get your grades done on time. Have you also noticed that you often have more patience with your students than you do with yourself? They can chat too much or miss an assignment, and most of the time you treat them in a kind and respectful way. How do you treat yourself when you run out of time, make a mistake on an administrative form, or forget to complete the attendance sheet? When do you become most irritated and impatient with yourself? How would you have treated another if they had made the same mistakes? Giving yourself a break from self-criticism is a wonderful gift.

"Patience is the companion of wisdom."

—St. Augustine

Exploration

"Life was meant to be lived, and curiosity must be kept alive.
One must never, for whatever reason, turn his back to life."

—Eleanor Roosevelt

When you watch small children begin to explore, they first go by inches and then by feet, always with a backward glance to see if Mom and Dad are still there. Soon they will bravely go to the curb and then across the street and on to school. They need to do this by degrees—baby steps growing into giant steps. Some children, as well as adults, move more quickly than others into the unknown and aren't happy unless it is a brand new frontier. Others see risk-taking as foolish and dangerous. We all must take some risks and be explorers. The practice of risk-taking and exploration opens our eyes, causing us to see the world in a new way. What new things have you explored in the last years? What lessons have you learned? What areas do you still want to explore?

"It does not matter how slowly you go, so long as you do not stop."

—Confucius

Fairies

Fairies live in an enchanted world, a place that children can easily visit. If you are a teacher of very young children, you see them enter the fairy world easily and frequently. If you teach older students, you probably have to create this enchanted world for them. In the early part of this century there were many fairy sightings. They were normally seen in gardens, wooded areas, or even hovering above the bed of someone who was deep within a dream. Because fairies live in different lands, they appear in different shapes and forms. Yet they all have one thing in common: they exist outside of our notion of time and space. People who believe in fairies, leprechauns, and other mythical creatures move into this dimension easily and experience true enchantment in their lives. Our children have much to teach us about this world.

Initiation

In most cultures of the world there is a moment when the youth are told, "You are no longer a child. You are now an adult." This initiation normally takes place with a complex ceremony filled with tests of strength and courage. A celebration concludes the ritual in order for the community to greet this new adult member of the tribe. In our culture we do not have an initiation ceremony that announces when a youth reaches maturity. Maybe this is why our youth stay half-child and half-adult for an extended time. When do they become adults? When they can drive, be drafted, or drink? How can we create a moment for our young that honors the passage from childhood into adulthood?

Magic

"Magic happens."

—Bumper Sticker

We all know the moment when magic happens in our classrooms. There might be a sudden hush, a cheer, or even applause. We can't make it happen, and often days, even weeks go by without a "magic moment." But when it does walk into our rooms, students feel it, we feel it, and at that moment we know why we are teachers. We must always be ready for magic so that we can let it become a spectacular event for everyone. When was the last time magic walked into your room?

"The teacher who is not afraid to make mistakes and who has a genuine respect for other people's ideas is filled with the energy from which classroom magic is made."

—Louise DeFelice

Jealousy

Jealousy can be a most dangerous emotion. It not only creates unbalance in our lives, but it also limits our feelings of self-worth. Jealously can be a form of greed; we don't want another to have the honor, the new classroom, or the advanced class because we want it and feel we deserve it. Some call this "petty jealousy," but no jealously is petty. It can eat away at us and cloud our ability to see our own gifts and talents. We know what jealousy feels like. It is an emotion that comes on quickly with strong bodily cues. When we feel it rising from within, it is good to look at our own special qualities with appreciation and be glad for another person's joy.

Manipulation

"O what a tangled web we weave, when first we practice to deceive."

—Sir Walter Scott

As teachers, we see obvious manipulative skills: tears, strong words, excuses, guilt. The harder ones to detect are kindness, sweetness, and smiles, and when these tricks come into play we often do not know that we have been manipulated until after the fact. We all become manipulative when we want things our way, even to the point that we are willing to compromise ourselves. Children are often manipulative because their ploys have worked so well in the past that they now perform them unconsciously. If we detect a child manipulating us, we should point out their unacceptable behavior and then show them more honest ways to achieve what they want. We must also look at our own manipulative behavior and become more truthful when we want another to behave in a specific way.

"Deal with faults of others as gently as with your own."

—Chinese Proverb

Treasures

"For where your treasure is, there will your heart be also."
—Matthew 6:21

Children are fascinated with stories of pirates burying treasure chests on sandy beaches in faraway places. Some of these chests might still exist, and treasure hunters are searching for them because they are believed to contain golden coins, gems, crowns of monarchs, and secrets of lost worlds. Our grandmothers had hope chests; many indigenous people have secret medicine bundles; and most of us have treasure boxes or drawers. These containers are filled with objects that tell about our pasts and indicate what gives us hope for the future. It is wise to check the contents of these precious containers frequently because inside are the treasures of our hearts.

"Memory is the diary we all carry around with us."
—Oscar Wilde

Lottery

"It would seem that you don't have any luck until you believe there is no such thing as luck at all."

—Irish Proverb

The lottery must be one of the ultimate "random acts of kindness." When there are winners, we carefully look at their photos in the newspaper to judge their worthiness. We look to see if they are too old, too young, or already too rich. We try to figure out why they had the winning numbers when it would have been fairer if we had received the millions of dollars. Winning the lottery is random luck, and as we experience more of life we realize how many events come about because of timing beyond our control. Sometimes we are winners, and sometimes we feel like losers. But generally these moments contain just the lesson we need at that point in our lives.

"Human life, its growth, its hopes, fear, loves et cetera, are the result of accident."

—Bertrand Russell

Weather

"Sunshine is delicious, rain is refreshing, wind braces us, snow is invigorating; there is no such thing as bad weather, only different kinds of good weather."

—John Ruskin

Each of us thrives on different kinds of weather. There are people who dry up in the sun and heat but relish misty, moist mornings. Others become depressed if the sun doesn't shine and want to retreat under covers when there is a thunderous rainstorm. Quickly changing weather can also affect us as teachers. We usually know before the weather forecaster when the barometric pressure is changing because our students seem plugged into invisible currents, and their behavior changes dramatically. Weather is just one of the many things we have to build into our day's activities. When thunder cracks and jolts our rooms and ends with a rainbow across the playground, or when snow builds up outside the building and students ask, "When will school be called off?", we need to revise our lesson plans quickly. We all need to enjoy the moments that nature gives us, so if you have a window, let the weather be a part of your classroom.

"I must confess to a feeling of profound humility in the presence of a universe which transcends us at almost every point."

—Isaac Newton

Tragedy

"If you learn from your suffering, and really come to understand the lesson you were taught, you might be able to help someone else . . . maybe that is what it is all about."

—Anonmyous

The ancient Greeks went to the theater to see tragedies in order to grow and be transformed. They were looking for what they called a "catharsis," or cleansing of the body and soul. When we are in the middle of a personal tragedy it is hard to believe that anything good might come from the experience. It is not until the immediate pain has passed that we discover how much we have learned and grown from the tragedy. Our students need to understand that when we go through difficult times, things will eventually return to normal, and tragic events can bring new and unexpected transformations. Which tragedy in your life produced the most growth?

"One may not reach the dawn save by the path of the night."

—Kahil Gibran

Violence

"Life only demands from you the strength you possess. Only one feat is possible, not to have to run away."

—Dag Hammarskjold

Teachers' jobs are now classified, along with postal workers, as hazardous and dangerous occupations. We are aware that our students' behavior is getting more and more violent, and it is hard to imagine the rage in a young person's soul that can erupt in such hateful acts. We cannot stop a child from stealing a weapon from his/her parent's gun cabinet, but we might develop better antennae to detect the child who has become so utterly lost within the system. There is no clear detection system, but we can't afford not to look deeply into the unhappy lives of some of our students.

"Life's under no obligation to give us what we expect."

—Margaret Mitchell

Space

"I would rather sit on a pumpkin, and have it all to myself, than to be crowded on a velvet cushion."

—Henry David Thoreau

How much personal space do you need to feel comfortable and secure? Each person has different spatial needs, which are often determined by cultural norms. In overpopulated countries and in large families, people get used to being comfortable in crowded situations. In schools that are over-enrolled, halls, cafeterias, and classrooms are so full that students and staff are jostled and jumbled throughout the day. Scientists have observed that animals in overcrowded laboratory cages become agitated and often violent when they are not given adequate space. We can do little about overcrowding in our building, but we can be aware that some of the stress we feel may come from too many people in too little space.

"The right to be left alone is indeed the beginning of all freedom."

—Justice William O. Douglas

Web

It's an interesting experience to walk slowly down a school corridor, stopping for a few seconds outside each open door. You have probably done this frequently and have experienced the invisible vibrations that emanate out of each classroom. If you could grab hold of one of these currents and follow it, hand over hand, you would find, at the other end, the teacher. We send our joy, enthusiasm, and love of the job into the room, and these are picked up by our students who, in turn, send out their interconnecting vibrations. Soon we have a gigantic three-dimensional web that we have spun together. The teacher is the master weaver who starts the process and therefore must be vigilant about what manner of web is being spun.

156

Roles

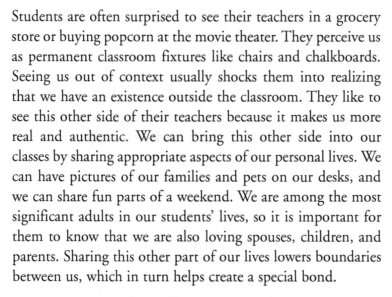

"Insist on yourself; never imitate."

—Ralph Waldo Emerson

Students are often surprised to see their teachers in a grocery store or buying popcorn at the movie theater. They perceive us as permanent classroom fixtures like chairs and chalkboards. Seeing us out of context usually shocks them into realizing that we have an existence outside the classroom. They like to see this other side of their teachers because it makes us more real and authentic. We can bring this other side into our classes by sharing appropriate aspects of our personal lives. We can have pictures of our families and pets on our desks, and we can share fun parts of a weekend. We are among the most significant adults in our students' lives, so it is important for them to know that we are also loving spouses, children, and parents. Sharing this other part of our lives lowers boundaries between us, which in turn helps create a special bond.

"Teachers generate magic when they stop thinking of themselves as teachers, and start thinking of themselves as human beings."

—Louise DeFelice

Maps

"The great thing in this world is not so much where we are going, but in what direction we are moving."

—Oliver Wendell Holmes

We have mapped almost every inch of the earth. The true adventurer, however, is one who goes into the unmapped and uncharted areas of our universe. Christopher Columbus went across the ocean without the benefit of a world map and mistakenly believed he had arrived in Asia. Lewis and Clark explored the American West, guided by Sacagawea, a young Native American woman who knew about the land only from childhood trips and stories. It's fun to set off on a drive without a plan or a map and let our intuition or the flip of a coin tell us which way to turn. In this manner we are bound to discover new villages, geological surprises, and historical sites that we would not have found if we had been bound to a map. How far would you go without a map? What is the most adventuresome thing you have done in your life? How long ago did you take this adventure? When do you plan another exploration into something new?

"If a man wishes to be sure of the road he treads on, he must close his eyes and walk in the dark."

—St. John of the Cross

Rules

"It's a poor rule that doesn't work in both ways."
—Frederick Douglass

"Rules are meant to be broken." This phrase definitely shows an understanding of human nature. Every day we see students testing the rules to see how far they can go before some form of enforcement takes place. The rules that are most apt to be broken are the ones that students do not understand and do not think necessary. Rules keep a community functioning smoothly and fairly, so it is imperative that students are given sound reasons why a rule has been made.

"Good laws mean more order."
—Aristotle

Markings

"That which we understand we cannot blame."

—Goethe

From the moment humans first walked on our planet they have had a need to leave their mark. They have felt it was imperative to paint, peck, and scratch the history of their people on the surfaces of cliffs and caves. The first markings were simple signs indicating hunts and migrations; then slowly they became more sophisticated symbols that told of abstract ideas and religious beliefs. We, too, have a need to leave our marks. Today we see them as graffiti on bathroom walls and indelible ink marks on student desks. These marks say, "I am here, this is how I feel, are you reading and listening to what I have to say?" Sometimes our students speak the loudest with these misplaced messages. We need to take the time to decipher what they are saying before we erase them. They are important clues as to what is on their minds, things they feel incapable or fearful of voicing aloud.

"Honesty and frankness make you vulnerable. Be honest and frank anyway."

—On the wall of Peet's Coffee Shop

Sacrifice

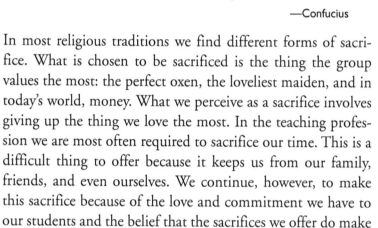

"If I am building a mountain and stop before the last basketfull of earth is placed on the summit, I have failed."

—Confucius

In most religious traditions we find different forms of sacrifice. What is chosen to be sacrificed is the thing the group values the most: the perfect oxen, the loveliest maiden, and in today's world, money. What we perceive as a sacrifice involves giving up the thing we love the most. In the teaching profession we are most often required to sacrifice our time. This is a difficult thing to offer because it keeps us from our family, friends, and even ourselves. We continue, however, to make this sacrifice because of the love and commitment we have to our students and the belief that the sacrifices we offer do make a difference.

"That which a man sacrifices is never lost"

—German Proverb

Community

"The whole idea of compassion is based on a keen awareness of interdependence of all living beings which are all part of one another and all involved in one another."

—Fr. Thomas Merton

What makes a community? It is a connectedness based on trust. This is a difficult thing to find in most institutions. What could you do today that might make a person in your building feel connected to a community? This person could be a student you pass in the hall, a parent you need to call, or the custodian who cleans the cafeteria for the hundredth time.

"Separate reeds are weak and easily broken, but bound together they are strong and hard to pull apart."

—The Midrash

Praise

"Praise is a kind of spiritual vitamin. Children, grownups, all of us, need it to be emotionally healthy."

—Stetson University

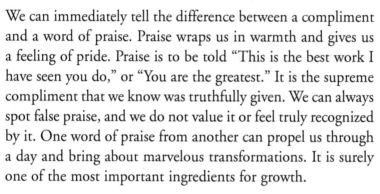

We can immediately tell the difference between a compliment and a word of praise. Praise wraps us in warmth and gives us a feeling of pride. Praise is to be told "This is the best work I have seen you do," or "You are the greatest." It is the supreme compliment that we know was truthfully given. We can always spot false praise, and we do not value it or feel truly recognized by it. One word of praise from another can propel us through a day and bring about marvelous transformations. It is surely one of the most important ingredients for growth.

"Say something nice to someone else and watch the world light up with joy."

—Anonymous

Seeds

"The seed never explains the flower."

—Edith Hamilton

There are many similarities between the job of a gardener and the job of a teacher. Both gardeners and teachers carefully prepare the soil, plant the seed, and then wait. Lucky gardeners will see the results of their work within a few weeks and enjoy glorious flowers and a bounteous crop of fruits and vegetables. Teachers, unfortunately, do not have this experience. They see spurts of growth but do not get to see the seeds grow to maturity. They know, however, that if they did their job, the seeds will reach their potential. Both of these occupations are based on a great amount of patience and hope for the future.

"In this world, things that are destined to endure a long time are the slowest to grow."

—St. Vincent de Paul

Moon

"I see the moon,
And the moon sees me.
God bless the moon,
and God bless me."
—Anonmyous

If we took the time to watch the waxing and waning of the moon for one month, we would better understand the significance of natural cycles. We have faith that the moon will return even though it totally disappears for several days each month. We have faith that the sun will rise in the east every morning and disappear in the western sky. When we lose faith in people and situations, we need to give the elements of nature a chance to renew our shaky belief and allow their reliability and beauty to renew our faith in our world.

"We are what we contemplate."

—Plato

Service

"Each citizen should play his part in the community according to his gifts."

—Plato

We were drawn to the teaching profession because there was a place inside of us that called us to serve the children. We feel rewarded by this life that allows us to give our knowledge, skills, and love to others. All life is sustained by the fact that we serve and, in turn, are served by others. Sometimes when we get caught up in the busyness of our jobs we forget that what we do is for the betterment of our world and the future. One of our obligations is to show our students not only the necessity but also the happiness that a life of service brings. We need to demonstrate that they are all significant strands in the interdependent web of life and that others truly need them.

"The only ones among you who will be really happy are those who have sought and found how to serve."

—Albert Schweitzer

Shadows

"I have a little shadow that goes in and out with me, and what can be the use of him is more than I can see."

—Robert Louis Stevenson

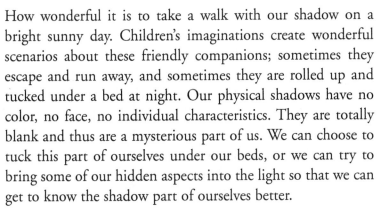

How wonderful it is to take a walk with our shadow on a bright sunny day. Children's imaginations create wonderful scenarios about these friendly companions; sometimes they escape and run away, and sometimes they are rolled up and tucked under a bed at night. Our physical shadows have no color, no face, no individual characteristics. They are totally blank and thus are a mysterious part of us. We can choose to tuck this part of ourselves under our beds, or we can try to bring some of our hidden aspects into the light so that we can get to know the shadow part of ourselves better.

"Wherever you go, you will always bear yourself about with you, and you will always find yourself."

—Thomas à Kempis

Smiles

"Never let anyone come to you without coming away better and happier. Everyone should see goodness in your face, your eyes, in your smile."

—Mother Teresa

How many different smiles do you have? You can often tell by watching the smiles that are given back to you. There are Mona Lisa smiles, Howdy Doody smiles, and Buddha smiles. A smile can be a tool for control, or it can be a great gift to someone. The Vietnamese Buddhist monk Thich Nhat Hanh encourages people to walk with a small contented smile on their faces because it will change the entire nature of a hike or stroll. Have you noticed how a smile from someone can change a difficult day? When you are given a smile you are likely to pass it on to someone else, and that person will in turn pass it on and on. . . .

"A smile goes a long way, but you're the one who must start it on its journey."

—Anonymous

Progress

"I walk slowly, but I never walk backward."

—Abraham Lincoln

When we fill out student reports and reflect on their growth, we never see a line continually ascending, but rather a line that moves backward at times before it spurts forward. Backward steps are inevitable parts of everyone's journey. Often these steps backward contain the greatest lessons and propel us forward. Sometimes looking at what we want to accomplish can bring a halt to our progress because it seems so huge and far away. If on the first day of school we tried to take in the entire school year and all we needed to accomplish, we would probably clean out our desks and walk away. We know that the best approach is to take it one day at a time so that our progress is manageable and enjoyable.

"The human mind always makes progress, but it is a progress of spirals."

—Madame de Stael

Souvenirs

*"And the king said, 'I shall never, never, forget.' 'You will though,'
said the Queen, 'if you don't make a memorandum of it.' "*

—Lewis Carroll

We collect souvenirs so that we will not forget special people
and places. Sometimes the memories that return when we see
or touch a momento are more wondrous and inspiring than
the actual experience. Often our favorite souvenirs are the sim-
plest ones: a Christmas tree ornament, a shell, or a postcard.
Our photo albums are important to us because we collect our
most wonderful memories in them. We have souvenirs in our
desk drawers at school that go back many years. Discovering
one school souvenir buried beneath paper clips and rubber
bands can bring back a flood of memories of special days, special students, and special activities. What are your favorite
school souvenirs? Have you given your students a souvenir so
that they will remember the year when you were their teacher?
What souvenir could you give your students this year that
would be a good reminder of the time that you had together?

*"One cannot collect all the beautiful shells on the beach. One
can collect only a few, and they are most beautiful if they are a
few."*

—Anne Morrow Lindbergh

Mirrors

"All the extraordinary men I have known were extraordinary in their own estimation."

—Woodrow Wilson

When we look into a mirror and see our reflections, we do not get an entirely accurate image; the lighting may have changed the color of our skin, and of course our face is seen in reverse. We also look to others for a reflection of who we are. We look into their eyes to see if they perceive us as competent, kind, or entertaining. What they reflect back is not always accurate because they see us through their unique pasts, needs, and desires. Because of our own insecurities we often take their perceptions to be accurate, which is a dangerous assumption. Reflections can be helpful because they help us adjust and correct our appearance and behavior, but we need to test their accuracy by using our own hearts and minds as guides.

"Cast off everything that is not yourself."

—Persius

Stones

"Everybody
needs a rock

I'm sorry for kids
who don't have
a rock
for a friend."

—Byrd Baylor

Throughout history people have delighted in the power and mystery of rocks and minerals. Small stones have been used by shamans and medicine people to bring health to individuals, and large stones have been dragged incredible distances to create holy sanctuaries. The Zunis of Arizona even have a medicine bundle in which they keep a stone that beats as a human heart. It is comforting to carry a stone in your pocket or have one on your desk. They can remind you of something you want to focus on that day: a friend, love, or patience. Children seem to understand the mystery of rocks and stones, and we often find a secret pile in their desks or closets.

"Anything will give up its secrets if you love it enough."

—George Washington Carver

The Moment

"Past and future are both contained in every present moment. Whatever we are today is the result of what we have thought and spoken and done in all the present moments before now—just as what we shall be tomorrow is the result of what we think, say, and do today."

—Eknath Easwaran

It is wise to live in the present moment, but it is often very difficult to leave our school building and drive home at night without thoughts of the past day or worries about tomorrow's lesson plans. Mystics suggest that having a mantra, a sacred or special word we repeat, will allow us to focus on the glorious present. Religious traditions suggest different mantras. Christians might use the name of Jesus; Hindus repeat Rama; and Buddhists cite "Om Mani Padme Hum," which means "jewel in the lotus of the heart." In the Jewish faith, "Barukh attah Adonai" is used, and many Muslims use "Allah." A mantra could be love, patience, peace, or light. Once you choose a word that seems right for you, stay with it. It's amazing how the power of concentrating on the sound of one word or phrase will keep you in the present and bring you peace, even on the drive home.

"The secret of health for both mind and body is not to mourn for the past, not to worry about the future, or not to anticipate troubles, but to live the present moment wisely and earnestly."

—The Buddha

Enthusiasm

"Exuberance is beauty."

—William Blake

When students were asked to identify the most important characteristics of an ideal teacher, enthusiasm was one of the most important attributes mentioned. Enthusiasm can be quiet and gentle, or it can be a boundless display of energy. The important thing is that it shows your students that you love what you are doing and that you love to share the world with them. Enthusiasm brings vibrancy into a room that is contagious; it creates miracles in relationships and in learning.

"Catch on fire with enthusiasm and people will come for miles to see you burn."

—John Wesley

Students

"He who learns, teaches "

—Ethiopian Proverb

When former students return for a visit, do you ever ask them what they remember most about your class? It's amazing what they will mention: a bulletin board display, a long-forgotten lecture, a remark of yours that you can't remember. These memories are mirrors that reflect the truly important moments in their education, and they can teach you a great deal about what kind of teacher you have been. We forget that our students can be our best teachers. Because they are younger and less experienced, we sometimes fail to see them as mentors who can guide us along our path. What are some of the greatest lessons your students have given you?

"Poor is the pupil who does not surpass his master."

—Leonardo da Vinci

Mountains

"The birds have vanished into the sky, and now the last cloud drains away. We sit together, the mountains and me, until only the mountains remain."

—Li Po

Weekends are very special because they are the times when we can escape from weekday stresses to become renewed. We all have our favorite escape places—a trout stream, a movie theater, a corner of our home. If you live near the mountains, you will probably go there when the weekend arrives. Mountains contain magic and mystery and are considered sacred sites by many people. They provide us with the ability not only to get away, but also to rise above our normal lives. This gives us the opportunity to gain a new perspective. On the top of a mountain our cities seem small, our neighborhoods inconsequential, and our schools invisible. A vantage point such as this shows us how immense our world is and how we are a part of one gigantic cosmic web.

"A monk asks: Is there anything more miraculous than the wonders of nature? The master answers: Yes, your awareness of nature."

—Hui Hai

Panic

"Make haste slowly."

—Augustus Caesar

Your heart skips a beat, your mouth is dry, and your mind races. Fortunately, panic doesn't occur often in a school year. But when it rushes through your door, you literally can become lost in the confusion. This is a most difficult situation. As a teacher, you must be the protector, guide, and guardian of your classroom. Taking a deep breath might help, but when you are in a panic mode this is hard to do. At times like this we need help from a colleague. We need to arrange for this kind of assistance throughout our building so we know that when a catastrophe hits, we are not alone.

"In union there is strength."

—Aesop

Talents

"Hide not your talents, they for use were made.
What's a sun-dial in the shade?"

—Benjamin Franklin

When we talk of someone's talents, we speak of their having gifts. When we receive talents, they carry with them commitment and responsibility to use these special qualities to help others. We need to praise and recognize the talents of all our students and help them see what fun it is to use their gifts to make the lives of others brighter and lighter.

"Perhaps our natural gifts elude us because they are so obvious."

—Sue Bender

178

Parents

"A father's goodness is higher than the mountains; a mother's goodness is deeper thatn the sea."

—Japanese Proverb

When we meet with parents, we get a deeper understanding of their children and also discover the amount of tenderness that surrounds our students in their homes. There are many parents whom we never meet, and the fact that they never visit the school does not mean that they do not love their children. Many simply do not have the social or economic resources to provide sufficient time for their children. We must remember that no person consciously chooses to be a bad parent. For children who have less time with their parents, we are a crucial part of their lives, and the extra time we can give them can make all the difference.

"The joys of parents are secret, and so are their grieves and fears."

—Francis Bacon

Surprises

"Even the predictable turns into surprise the moment we stop taking it for granted."

—Br. David Steindl-Rast

Each morning we take off our coats, check our mailboxes, rearrange the chairs, and prepare ourselves for nine hours of surprises. Surprises can be fun, or they can test our patience to the limit, but would we really want a day without at least one? The exciting thing about surprises is that they have a life of their own. We have little, if any, control over their beginning or end. All we can do is see them as gifts, rejoice in them, learn from them, and be grateful that there is little boredom in the life of a teacher.

"If we do not expect the unexpected, we will never find it."

—Heraclitus

Lies

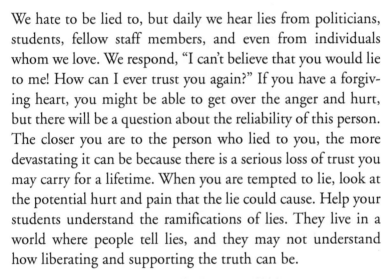

"Never forget a half truth is as a whole lie."

—Anonymous

We hate to be lied to, but daily we hear lies from politicians, students, fellow staff members, and even from individuals whom we love. We respond, "I can't believe that you would lie to me! How can I ever trust you again?" If you have a forgiving heart, you might be able to get over the anger and hurt, but there will be a question about the reliability of this person. The closer you are to the person who lied to you, the more devastating it can be because there is a serious loss of trust you may carry for a lifetime. When you are tempted to lie, look at the potential hurt and pain that the lie could cause. Help your students understand the ramifications of lies. They live in a world where people tell lies, and they may not understand how liberating and supporting the truth can be.

"One lie gives birth to another."

—Terence

Teams

"A single bracelet does not jingle."

—African Saying

We have all been placed in teams in our school. The underlying principle is that more people can create and accomplish more. In reality, however, we know that we just can't take individuals, put them in the same environment, and make them into a team. There are two important ingredients for making a group of people into a cohesive and successful team: respect and trust. Being a part of a group that isn't a true team can prevent people from becoming the teachers they want to be. On the other hand, being a part of an accomplished team can bring miracles into a school building. When we are put on a team, we must remain open to the fact that this new circle, although difficult to form, might make a difference in our teaching career. When people interconnect for the purpose of helping others, amazing and unexpected things can happen.

"Teamwork is the ability to work together for a common vision.
It is a fuel that allows the common people to attain uncommon
results."

—Anonymous

Medicine

*"When the wind blows,
    that is my medicine.
When it rains,
    that is my medicine.
When it hails,
    that is my medicine.
When it becomes clear after a storm,
    that is my medicine."*

—Anonymous

To most of us, medicines are drops and pills we must take to improve our physical health. To Native Americans, however, medicine refers to the personal power that each person possesses. They use the term "good medicine," which refers to one's inner power to heal individuals and a community. As teachers, we cannot dispense medicine to our students, but there is nothing to stop us from making them feel better with healing words and touch. Sometimes all a headache needs is caring concern, and an upset stomach can disappear with a few words of sympathy. We are often the first person students run to with their bumps and bruises. They understand that the best medicine can be our healing love and concern.

"The main reason for healing is love."

—Paracelsus

Thank Yous

"Gratitude is the heart's memory."

—French Proverb

As a student was leaving a classroom one day, he turned to his teacher and softly whispered, "Thanks." The surprised teacher looked up and asked, "What for?" The student responded, "For today's great class." The unexpected "thank you" that comes out of nowhere has to be one of the greatest gifts in the world. It's good to thank a person who has gone out of his or her way to help you, but the unanticipated thank you that flows spontaneously from the heart is an unexpected gift that makes the world a kinder and more gentle place.

"Swift gratitude is the sweetest."

—Greek Proverb

Lifeline

"History is a child building a sandcastle by the sea, and that child is the whole majesty of man's power in the world."
—Heraclitus

Your lifeline is as unique as your fingerprints. It is important to stop once in awhile to take a close look at where you have been. If you have a few minutes, you might want to try this simple activity. (It's also fun to do with students.) Draw a horizontal line across a piece of paper, and on the left end write the date of your birthday, and on the right end, today's date. Next, place along the line significant events in your life. Now look at your high points and low points. You are ready to make a life graph by marking a dot above or below the line for each event. If it was a really high point, it might be two inches above the line. If it was a major crisis, the dot would fall far below the line. If the event was not too significant, it might rest on the horizontal line. Now connect the dots. When you have completed this activity, examine your life and see how much this simple graph can show you. One lesson that becomes obvious is that no matter how far below the line an event may fall, there is always a return to normalcy. It may even be that the most difficult moment led to one of the highest peaks of your life.

"Study the past, if you would divine the future."
—Confucius

Threats

"What stirs your anger when done to you by others, that do not do to others."

—Socrates

Threats are dangerous. We hear them every day in the halls, on the playground, and in classrooms. We have all been threatened verbally, if not physically, by a student, and we know how unsettling and even frightening it can be. Most often we did not deserve the threat that bubbled up and out of a child, and most likely other people or events in the child's life brought on the strong words and cruel looks. As victims, we often become paralyzed and angry that we have been treated in such a cruel and unjust manner. As teachers, we are also tempted to use verbal threats, though in most cases little can be accomplished with this type of behavior. It is much better to use a "cooling off" period and then negotiate a peace.

"Words gain credibility by deeds."

—Terence

Moods

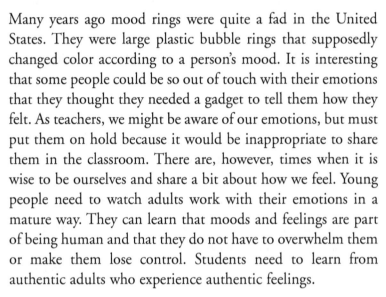

"It is terribly amusing how many climates of feeling one can go through in a day."

—Anne Morrow Linbergh

Many years ago mood rings were quite a fad in the United States. They were large plastic bubble rings that supposedly changed color according to a person's mood. It is interesting that some people could be so out of touch with their emotions that they thought they needed a gadget to tell them how they felt. As teachers, we might be aware of our emotions, but must put them on hold because it would be inappropriate to share them in the classroom. There are, however, times when it is wise to be ourselves and share a bit about how we feel. Young people need to watch adults work with their emotions in a mature way. They can learn that moods and feelings are part of being human and that they do not have to overwhelm them or make them lose control. Students need to learn from authentic adults who experience authentic feelings.

"Once you are Real you can't be unreal again. It lasts for always."

—Margery Williams
The Velveteen Rabbit

Timing

"An impatient person is not fit to teach."

—The Talmud

Much of the success in our personal lives and in our classrooms comes from good timing—for instance, the best moment to ask a family member to do a chore or when to tell a student about a problem that you feel needs to be dealt with. If we aren't aware of how the other person is feeling emotionally and physically at the time of our request, we will be ignored or become the cause of a further conflict. We are so often on our own schedule that we lose our ability to be sensitive to other people's needs. If we are attentive, cautious, and aware, we will be able to master the art of timing and be able to reach our goals graciously and with kindness.

"True mastery can be gained by letting things go their own way. It can't be gained by interfering."

—Lao Tzu

188

Wise Ones

"I hope I never get too old to listen to advice from a wise person."

—Socrates

The wise individuals in our lives are those who know how to listen carefully and are slow to give advice. There is a Tibetan proverb that says, "The wise ones are the servants of all." In Tibet, people of wisdom are never paid for their services because they view their wisdom as a blessing and thus have an obligation to share it with all. In a culture that pays top dollar for outside consultants and experts in the field, we forget that sometimes the best advice can be free.

"Wisdom is like having a thousand eyes."

—Tibetan Proverb

Tradition

"Now join your hands and with your hands your hearts."
—William Shakespeare

If we are to understand another culture, we must take a careful look at the traditions that have been handed down through countless generations. Tradition is the glue that holds a community together. Some experts believe that the confusion we find in today's youth comes from the disappearance of our traditions. A high school history teacher was saddened one day when she was discussing the story of George Washington cutting down the cherry tree to discover that not one of her twenty-eight juniors knew this classic American story. We celebrate many traditional holidays, and yet few Americans know much about the person or event that is being honored. When our youth do not feel a bond with their culture or their family, they may search for membership in another group that might not have ethical goals or values. Schools need to find ways to reach out to all youth who are looking for traditions and a place to belong.

"Tradition does not mean that the living are dead, but that the dead are living."

—G. K. Chesterton

"Yes"

"Whatever I have tried to do in my life, I have always tried with all my heart to do it well; whatever I have devoted myself to, I have devoted myself to it completely."

—Charles Dickens

Sometimes responding "yes" to a request is easy: "Yes, I will be on your committee." Other times a "yes" can be almost overwhelming to say: "Yes, I will marry you." Every "yes" statement, whether large or small, requires an enormous commitment. You are promising to be there no matter what! It is wise to be thoughtful and hesitant about saying "yes," because once you have said the word you must be committed, loyal, and available.

"A person with half volition goes backwards and forwards, but makes no progress even on the smoothest of roads."

—Thomas Carlyle

Memories

"The true art of memory is attention."

—Samuel Adams

Snapshot moments are the memories that are so imprinted on our minds that we can recall every detail of a scene, even though it happened many years ago. Some of those moments were joy-filled; others were traumatic. Nevertheless, they are the events that define who we are. Remember to open your internal photo album frequently to relive the joys and sorrows that made you the person you are today. What are your favorite snapshot moments?

"Memory is the cabinet of imagination."

—Basile

Wedding

"Look down, you gods, and on this couple drop a blessed crown."

—William Shakespeare

We are all deeply moved when we witness two people pledge to love each other for the rest of their lives. It is wonderful to watch children at a wedding. Their eyes are wide and bright as they watch a beautiful princess and a handsome bridegroom make their vows. As adult guests, we hope that the promises we are witnessing will be kept, but we also wonder if this marriage will last and whether the love will continue. We live in a world of changing values and lifestyles that threaten the permanence of any institution. Weddings are opportunities for us to look deeply into our hearts and remember all the promises and commitments we have made.

"Two souls and one thought, two hearts and one pulse."

—Halen

Farewell

"I can generally bear the separation, but I don't like the leave-taking."

—Samuel Butler

We anticipate spring, knowing that soon we will have a vacation to restore the body and soul. However, we are approaching the time when we must say farewell to our students, to whom we have tirelessly committed ourselves for nine months. There were days when we could think only of the freedom of summer. But now as the last days approach, we realize how hard it is to say farewell. Our students will come back to visit, some even with their babies in their arms, but the circle that we created during the school year will disperse, never to be put back in the same way again. Our year together is over, but our influence and love will move out with each of our students into eternity. How lucky we are to be able to touch the stars that light the future.

"Light tomorrow with today."

—Elizabeth Barrett Browning

194

Adventure

"The big question is whether you are going to be able to say a hearty 'yes' to your adventure."

—Joseph Campbell

If you won a travel prize that covered all expenses along with a paid two-month leave from school, where would you go? Would you choose a secluded beach in Tahiti, a sacred site such as Machu Pichu, a climbing expedition in the Himalayas, or perhaps a little cabin just a few miles from where you live? We all have different travel dreams, some of us even preferring to stay at home and be "arm chair" travelers. Whether we are adventurers who love taking risks or we are happy in our nests, we must remember that new experiences make us wiser and more stimulating teachers.

"Life is either a daring adventure or nothing."

—Helen Keller

Happiness

"Most people are as happy as they make up their minds to be."

—Abraham Lincoln

List twenty things that make you happy. Go through your list and mark those that you like to do alone, with a group, or with a special person. Now go through and mark those that cost more than twenty dollars; also note which ones are absolutely free. Finally go through the list and try to remember the last time you did each activity. Many people are amazed to see how little room they make in their lives for the things that bring them the most joy. Don't let one more day go by without doing something that makes you very happy.

> *"Happiness is a butterfly which, when pursued, is always just beyond your grasp, but which, if you sit down quietly, may alight on you."*
>
> —Nathaniel Hawthorne

Toys

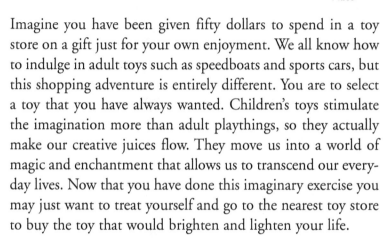

"You can discover more about a person in an hour of play than in a year of conversation."

—Plato

Imagine you have been given fifty dollars to spend in a toy store on a gift just for your own enjoyment. We all know how to indulge in adult toys such as speedboats and sports cars, but this shopping adventure is entirely different. You are to select a toy that you have always wanted. Children's toys stimulate the imagination more than adult playthings, so they actually make our creative juices flow. They move us into a world of magic and enchantment that allows us to transcend our everyday lives. Now that you have done this imaginary exercise you may just want to treat yourself and go to the nearest toy store to buy the toy that would brighten and lighten your life.

"It takes a long time to become young."

—Pablo Picasso

Reunion

"To part is to die a little."

—Anonymous

Imagine having a reunion of all the students you have ever taught. It would certainly be an impossible task to recognize all the faces altered by time and age. Some you would recognize instantly. Others might say, "You probably don't remember me, but you were my favorite teacher, and I now have my own classroom because of you." It's difficult for us to comprehend the influence we can have on one person's life. It's sad that we can't reconnect with many of our students. There would be many who would say, "You changed my life. Thank you."

"The blossom cannot tell what becomes of its odor, and no man can tell what becomes of his influence and example."

—Henry Ward Beecher

Topical Index

Bibliography

Andrews, Robert. *Columbia Dictionary of Quotations.* New York: Columbia University Press, 1993.

Ashton-Warner, Sylvia. *Myself.* New York: Simon and Schuster, 1967.

Aurelius, Marcus. *Meditations.* Translated by George Long. Buffalo, NY: Prometheus Books, 1991.

Bartlett, John. *Familiar Quotations.* 14th ed. Boston: Little, Brown & Co., 1968.

Barrie, J. M. *Peter Pan.* New York: Bantam Book, 1985.

Baylor, Byrd. *When Clay Sings.* New York: Aladdin Paperbacks, 1985.

———. *Everyone Needs a Rock.* New York: Aladdin Paperbacks, 1985.

Beecher, Henry Ward. *Selections from the Works of Henry Ward Beecher.* Boston: Caldwell, 1902.

Bender, Sue. *Everyday Sacred.* San Francisco: HarperSanFrancisco, 1995.

———. *Plain and Simple: A Women's Journey to Amish Country.* San Francisco: Harper & Row, 1989.

Blake, William. *Marriage of Heaven and Hell.* New York: E. P. Dutton & Co., 1927.

———. *Songs of Innocence and Songs of Experience.* Edited by Andrew Lincoln. Princeton, NJ: William Blake Trust/Princeton University Press, 1991.

Campbell, Joseph, and Bill Moyers. *The Power of Myth.* Edited by Betty Sue Flowers. New York: Doubleday, 1988.

Carroll, Lewis. *Alice Through the Looking Glass.* New York: Doubleday, 1982.

Chesterton, G. K. *Stories, Essays, and Poems.* Everyman's Library: Essays & Belles-lettres, no. 913. London: J. M. Dent & Sons, 1935.

———. *Tremendous Trifles.* New York: Dodd, Mead & Co., 1922.

Chodron, Pema. *Awakening Loving-Kindness.* Boston: Shambhala, 1996.

———. *The Wisdom of No Escape.* Boston: Shambhala, 1991.

Clemens, Samuel. *Mark Twain's Notebook.* New York: Cooper Square, 1972.

Collison, Robert, and Mary Collison, ed. *Dictionary of Foreign Quotations.* New York: Facts on File, 1980.

Dalai Lama. *The Dalai Lama's Book of Wisdom.* New York: Thorson, 2000.

———. *The Essential Teachings: His Holiness the Dalai Lama.* Berkeley: North Atlantic Press, 1995.

———. *The Path of Tranquillity.* New York: Viking, 1999.

DeFelice, Louise. "The Bibbidiboddidiboo Factor in Teaching". *Phi Delta Kappan,* April 1989.

Easwaran, Eknath. *Conquest of the Mind.* Petaluma, CA: Nilgiri Press, 1988.

———. *Words to Live By.* Petaluma, CA: Nilgiri Press, 1996.

———. *Your Life is Your Message.* New York: Hyperian, 1992.

Edberg, Rolf. *On the Shred of a Cloud.* Translated by Sven Ahman. Tuscaloosa, AL: University of Alabama Press, 1969.

Einstein, Albert. *Ideas and Opinions.* New York: Crown Publisher, 1954.

———. *The World As I See It.* New York: Carol Publishing Group, 1999.

———. *The Quotable Einstein.* Collected and Edited by Alice Calaprice. Princeton, NJ: Princeton University Press, 1996.

Emerson, Ralph Waldo. *The Complete Writings of Ralph Waldo Emerson.* New York: Wm. H. Wise & Co., 1929.

Farber, Bernard E., comp. *A Teacher's Treasury of Quotes.* Jefferson, NC: McFarland & Co., Ind., Publishers, 1985.

Fischer, Louis, ed. *The Essential Gandhi: An Anthology His Life, Work, and Ideas.* New York: Vintage Books, 1962.

Forster, E. M. *Where Angels Fear to Tread.* London: Edward Arnold, 1975.

Frank, Anne. *Diary of a Young Girl.* New York: Modern Library, 1952.

Frost, Robert. *Robert Frost's Poems.* New York: The Pocket Library, 1956.

Gandhi, Mohandas K. *An Autobiography: The Story of My Experiments With Truth.* Boston: Beacon Hill, 1957.

———. *All Men are Brothers: The Life and Thoughts of Mahatma Gandhi As Told in His Words.* Edited by Krishna Kripalani. Paris: Unesco Publications, 1958.

Gibran, Kahil. *The Prophet.* New York: Knopf, 1966.

———. *A Treasury of Kahil Gibran.* Edited by Martin L. Wolf. New York: The Citadel Press, 1954.

Glasser, William. *Positive Addiction.* New York: HarperCollins, 1985.

Goethe, Johann Wolfgang von. *The Permanent Goethe.* New York: Dial Press, 1948.

Halifax, Joan. *The Fruitful Darkness.* New York: HarperCollins, 1993.

Hammarskjold, Dag. *Markings.* New York: Knopf, 1964.

Holmes, Oliver Wendell. *Complete Poetical Works of Oliver Wendell Holmes.* New York: Houghton, 1910.

Keating, Thomas. *Active Meditations for Contemplative Prayer.* New York: Continuum, 1997.

———. *Invitation to Love.* New York: Continuum, 1999.

———. *Open Mind, Open Heart.* New York: Continuum, 1997.

Keller, Helen. *The Story of My Life.* New York: Doubleday Page & Co., 1903.

———. *Teacher: Anne Sullivan Macy.* Garden City, NY: Doubleday, 1955.

Krishnamurti, Jiddu. *Think On These Things.* New York: Harper & Row, 1964.

Lame Deer, John, and Richard Erdoes. *Lame Deer Seeker of Visions.* New York: Washington Square Press, 1972.

Lao Tze. *Tao te ching.* New York: harper and Row, 1988.

Lin, Yutang. *The Importance of Living.* New York: W. Morrow, 1996.

Lindbergh, Ann Morrow. *Gifts From the Sea.* New York: Pantheon Books, 1977.

———. *War Within and Without: Diaries and Letters of Anne Morrow Lindbergh 1935-1955.* San Diego: Harcourt Brace, 1995.

Lowell, James Russell. *Essays: English and American.* New York: P. F. Collier & Sons, 1938.

Macmillan Publishing Company. *Macmillan Dictionary of Quotations.* New York: Macmillan, 1989.

Marke, Julius J., ed. *Holmes Reader.* New York: Oceana Publications, 1955.

May, Rollo. *Man's Search for Himself.* New York: Bantam Doubleday Dell, 1953.

Merton, Thomas. *A Search for Solitude: Pursuing the Monk's True Life.* San Francisco: HarperSanFrancisco, 1996.

———. *New Seeds of Contemplation.* New York: New Directions Book, 1961.

Metzger, Deena. *Writing for Your Life.* San Francisco: HarperSanFrancisco, 1992.

Mother Teresa. *In the Heart of the World: Thoughts, Stories, and Prayers.* Novato, CA: New World Library, 1997.

———. *In My Own Words.* Thorndike, ME: G. K. Hall, 1996.

———. *No Greater Love.* Novato, CA: New World Library, 1997.

Moulthrop, Glenna Hammer. *Living in Love: A Compilation of Mother Teresa's Teachings on Love.* Nashville: Towle House Publishing Co., 2000.

Murphy, Edward F., ed. *The Crown Treasure of Relevant Quotations.* New York: Crown Publishers, Inc., 1978.

Niehardt, John G. *Black Elk Speaks.* New York: Pocket Books, 1972.

Olson, Sigurd. *Listening Point.* New York: Knopf, 1958.

Osbon, Diane, ed. *Joseph Campbell Reader.* New York: HarperCollins, 1991.

Rinpoche, Sogyal. *Glimpse After Glimpse.* Edited by Patrick Gaffney. San Francisco: HarperSanFrancisco, 1995.

Rogers, Carl. *Freedom to Learn.* Columbus, OH: C. E. Merrill Publishing Co., 1969.

———. *On Becoming a Person.* Boston: Houghton Mifflin, 1961.

Roosevelt, Eleanor. *On My Own.* New York: Harper, 1958.

————. *This is My Story*. New York: Harper & Brothers, 1937.

————. *What I Hope to Leave Behind: The Essential Essays of Eleanor Roosevelt*. Edited by Allida M. Black. Brooklyn: Carlson Publishers, 1995.

Safranshy, Sy, ed. *Sunbeams: A Book of Quotations*. Berkeley, CA: North Atlantic Press, 1990.

Saint-Exupéry, Antoine de. *The Little Prince*. New York: Harcourt-Brace, 1943.

————. *Wind, Sand, and Stars*. New York: Harbrace, 1939.

Schweitzer, Albert. *Out of My Life and Thought: An Autobiography*. New York: H. Hold, 1949.

————. *The Wit and Wisdom of Albert Schweitzer*. Boston: Beacon Press, 1949.

Settel, Trudy, comp. *The Wisdom of Gandhi*. New York: Philosophical Library, 1967.

Shakespeare, William. *Complete Works*. Edited by Stanley Wells and Gary Taylor. Oxford: Clarendon Press, 1986.

Steindl-Rast, David. *Gratefulness: The Heart of Prayer*. New York: Paulist Press, 1984.

Stevenson, Robert-Louis. *A Child's Garden of Verses*. San Francisco: Chroncile Books, 1989.

————. *A Listening Heart: The Art of Contemplation*. New York: Crossroad, 1988.

Sutton, Joseph, ed. *Words of Wellness*. Carson, CA: Hay House Inc., 1991.

Thomas à Kempis. *The Imitation of Christ*. Transated by William Benham. New York: PF Collier, 1909.

Thich Nhat Hanh. *Breathe! You Are Alive*. Berkeley, CA: Parallax Press, 1996.

————. *A Guide to Walking Meditation*. Berkeley, CA: Parallax Press, 1985.

————. *Peace in Every Step: The Path of Mindfulness in Everyday Life*. New York: Bantam Books, 1992.

————. *Present Moment, Wonderful Moment*. Berkeley, CA: Parallax Press, 1990.

Thondup, Tulku, and Daniel P. Goleman. *The Healing Power of Mind: Mediation Exercises for Health, Well Being, and Enlightenment*. Boston: Shambhala, 1996.

Thoreau, Henry David. *Walden and Other Writings*. Modern Library, Edited by Brooks Atkinson, no. 155. New York: Modern Library, 1965.

————. *Journal of Henry David Thoreau*. Edited by Bradford Torry and Francis H. Allen. Boston: Houghton Mifflin, 1949.

Travers, P. L. *Mary Poppins*. San Diego: Harcourt Brace Jovanovich, 1985.

Van Matre, Steve, and Bill Weiler, ed. *The Earth Speaks*. Greenville, WV: The Institute for Earth Education, 1994.

Wall, Steve and Harvey Arden. *Wisdom Keepers*. Hillsboro, OR: Beyond Words Publishing, 1990.

White, E. B. *Charlotte's Web*. New York: Harper/Econ/Perma, 1980.

Whitman, Walt. *Complete Poetry and Collected Prose*. New York: Viking Press, 1982.

————. *Leaves of Grass*. New York: Doubleday Doran & Co., Inc., 1940.

Wilde, Oscar. *Complete Works of Oscar Wilde*. London: Collins, 1966.

————. *The Importance of Being Earnest and Other Plays*. New York: New American Library, 1985.

Williams, Margery. *Velveteen Rabbit*. New York: Knopf, 1985.

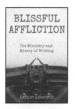

Choosing Gratitude
Learning to Love the Life You Have

James A. Autry

Autry reminds us that gratitude is a choice, a spiritual—not social—process. He suggests that if we cultivate gratitude as a way of being, we may not change the world and its ills, but we can change our response to the world. If we fill our lives with moments of gratitude, we will indeed love the life we have.   *978-1-57312-614-4 144 pages/pb* **$15.00**

Choosing Gratitude 365 Days a Year
Your Daily Guide to Grateful Living

James A. Autry and Sally J. Pederson

Filled with quotes, poems, and the inspired voices of both Pederson and Autry, in a society consumed by fears of not having "enough"— money, possessions, security, and so on—this book suggests that if we cultivate gratitude as a way of being, we may not change the world and its ills, but we can change our response to the world.   *978-1-57312-689-2 210 pages/pb* **$18.00**

Contextualizing the Gospel
A Homiletic Commentary on 1 Corinthians

Brian L. Harbour

Harbour examines every part of Paul's letter, providing a rich resource for those who want to struggle with the difficult texts as well as the simple texts, who want to know how God's word—all of it—intersects with their lives today.   *978-1-57312-589-5 240 pages/pb* **$19.00**

Dance Lessons
Moving to the Beat of God's Heart

Jeanie Miley

Miley shares her joys and struggles a she learns to "dance" with the Spirit of the Living God.   *978-1-57312-622-9 240 pages/pb* **$19.00**

A Divine Duet
Ministry and Motherhood

Alicia Davis Porterfield, ed.

Each essay in this inspiring collection is as different as the mother-minister who wrote it, from theologians to chaplains, inner-city ministers to rural-poverty ministers, youth pastors to preachers, mothers who have adopted, birthed, and done both.

978-1-57312-676-2 146 pages/pb **$16.00**

The Enoch Factor
The Sacred Art of Knowing God
Steve McSwain

The Enoch Factor is a persuasive argument for a more enlightened
religious dialogue in America, one that affirms the goals of all
religions—guiding followers in self-awareness, finding serenity
and happiness, and discovering what the author describes as "the sacred art of
knowing God." 978-1-57312-556-7 256 pages/pb **$21.00**

Ethics as if Jesus Mattered
Essays in Honor of Glen H. Stassen
Rick Axtell, Michelle Tooley, Michael L. Westmoreland-White, eds.

Ethics as if Jesus Mattered will introduce Stassen's work to a new
generation, advance dialogue and debate in Christian ethics, and
inspire more faithful discipleship just as it honors one whom the
contributors consider a mentor. 978-1-57312-695-3 234 pages/pb **$18.00**

Healing Our Hurts
Coping with Difficult Emotions
Daniel Bagby

In *Healing Our Hurts*, Daniel Bagby identifies and explains all the
dynamics at play in these complex emotions. Offering practical
biblical insights to these feelings, he interprets faith-based responses
to separate overly religious piety from true, natural human emotion. This book
helps us learn how to deal with life's difficult emotions in a redemptive and
responsible way. 978-1-57312-613-7 144 pages/pb **$15.00**

Help! I Teach Youth Sunday School
Brian Foreman, Bo Prosser, and David Woody

Real-life stories are mingled with information on Youth and their
culture, common myths about Sunday School, a new way of preparing the Sunday school lesson, creative teaching ideas, ways to think
about growing a class, and how to reach out for new members and
reach in to old members. 1-57312-427-3 128 pages/pb **$14.0**

Hope for the Thinking Christian
Seeking a Path of Faith through Everyday Life
Stephen Reese

Readers who want to confront their faith more directly, to think it
through and be open to God in an individual, authentic, spiritual
encounter will find a resonant voice in Stephen Reese.

978-1-57312-553-6 160 pages/pb **$16.00**

A Hungry Soul Desperate to Taste God's Grace
Honest Prayers for Life
Charles Qualls

Part of how we *see* God is determined by how we *listen* to God. There is so much noise and movement in the world that competes with images of God. This noise would drown out God's beckoning voice and distract us. Charles Qualls's newest book offers readers prayers for that journey toward the meaning and mystery of God.   *978-1-57312-648-9 152 pages/pb* **$14.00**

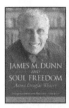

James M. Dunn and Soul Freedom
Aaron Douglas Weaver

James Milton Dunn, over the last fifty years, has been the most aggressive Baptist proponent for religious liberty in the United States. Soul freedom—voluntary, uncoerced faith and an unfettered individual conscience before God—is the basis of his understanding of church-state separation and the historic Baptist basis of religious liberty.   *978-1-57312-590-1 224 pages/pb* **$18.00**

The Jesus Tribe
Following Christ in the Land of the Empire
Ronnie McBrayer

The Jesus Tribe fleshes out the implications, possibilities, contradictions, and complexities of what it means to live within the Jesus Tribe and in the shadow of the American Empire.

978-1-57312-592-5 208 pages/pb **$17.00**

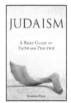

Judaism
A Brief Guide to Faith and Practice
Sharon Pace

Sharon Pace's newest book is a sensitive and comprehensive introduction to Judaism. What is it like to be born into the Jewish community? How does belief in the One God and a universal morality shape the way in which Jews see the world? How does one find meaning in life and the courage to endure suffering? How does one mark joy and forge community ties?   *978-1-57312-644-1 144 pages/pb* **$16.00**

Lessons from the Cloth 2
501 More One Minute Motivators for Leaders
Bo Prosser and Charles Qualls

As the force that drives organizations to accomplishment, leadership is at a crucial point in churches, corporations, families, and almost every arena of life. In this follow-up to their first volume, Prosser and Qualls will inspire you to keep growing in your leadership career.

978-1-57312-665-6 152 pages/pb **$11.00**

Let Me More of Their Beauty See
Reading Familiar Verses in Context
Diane G. Chen

Let Me More of Their Beauty See offers eight examples of how attention to the historical and literary settings can safeguard against taking a text out of context, bring out its transforming power in greater dimension, and help us apply Scripture appropriately in our daily lives.

978-1-57312-564-2 160 pages/pb **$17.00**

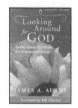

Looking Around for God
The Strangely Reverent Observations of an Unconventional Christian
James A. Autry

Looking Around for God, Autry's tenth book, is in many ways his most personal. In it he considers his unique life of faith and belief in God. Autry is a former Fortune 500 executive, author, poet, and consultant whose work has had a significant influence on leadership thinking.

978-157312-484-3 144 pages/pb **$16.00**

Making the Timeless Word Timely
A Primer for Preachers
Michael B. Brown

Michael Brown writes, "There is a simple formula for sermon preparation that creates messages that apply and engage whether your parish is rural or urban, young or old, rich or poor, five thousand members or fifty." The other part of the task, of course, involves being creative and insightful enough to know how to take the general formula for sermon preparation and make it particular in its impact on a specific congregation. Brown guides the reader through the formula and the skills to employ it with excellence and integrity.

978-1-57312-578-9 160 pages/pb **$16.00**

Meeting Jesus Today
For the Cautious, the Curious, and the Committed
Jeanie Miley

Meeting Jesus Today, ideal for both individual study and small groups, is intended to be used as a workbook. It is designed to move readers from studying the Scriptures and ideas within the chapters to recording their journey with the Living Christ.

978-1-57312-677-9 320 pages/pb **$19.00**

The Ministry Life
101 Tips for New Ministers
John Killinger

Sharing years of wisdom from more than fifty years in ministry and teaching, *The Ministry Life: 101 Tips for New Ministers* by John Killinger is filled with practical advice and wisdom for a minister's day-to-day tasks as well as advice on intellectual and spiritual habits to keep ministers of any age healthy and fulfilled. 978-1-57312-662-5 244 pages/pb **$19.00**

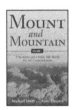

Mount and Mountain
Vol. 1: A Reverend and a Rabbi Talk About the Ten Commandments
Rami Shapiro and Michael Smith

Mount and Mountain represents the first half of an interfaith dialogue—a dialogue that neither preaches nor placates but challenges its participants to work both singly and together in the task of reinterpreting sacred texts. Mike and Rami discuss the nature of divinity, the power of faith, the beauty of myth and story, the necessity of doubt, the achievements, failings, and future of religion, and, above all, the struggle to live ethically and in harmony with the way of God. 978-1-57312-612-0 144 pages/pb **$15.00**

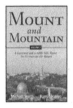

Mount and Mountain
Vol. 2: A Reverend and a Rabbi Talk About the Sermon on the Mount
Rami Shapiro and Michael Smith

This book, focused on the Sermon on the Mount, represents the second half of Mike and Rami's dialogue. In it, Mike and Rami explore the text of Jesus' sermon cooperatively, contributing perspectives drawn from their lives and religious traditions and seeking moments of illumination. 978-1-57312-654-0 254 pages/pb **$19.00**

Overcoming Adolescence
Growing Beyond Childhood into Maturity
Marion D. Aldridge

In *Overcoming Adolescence*, Marion D. Aldridge poses questions for adults of all ages to consider. His challenge to readers is one he has personally worked to confront: to grow up *all the way*—mentally, physically, academically, socially, emotionally, and spiritually. The key involves not only knowing how to work through the process but also how to recognize what may be contributing to our perpetual adolescence.

978-1-57312-577-2 156 pages/pb **$17.00**

To order call **1-800-747-3016** or visit **www.helwys.com**

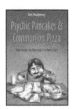

Psychic Pancakes & Communion Pizza
More Musings and Mutterings of a Church Misfit
Bert Montgomery

Psychic Pancakes & Communion Pizza is Bert Montgomery's highly anticipated follow-up to *Elvis, Willie, Jesus & Me* and contains further reflections on music, film, culture, life, and finding Jesus in the midst of it all.   *978-1-57312-578-9 160 pages/pb* **$16.00**

Quiet Faith
An Introvert's Guide to Spiritual Survival
Judson Edwards

In eight finely crafted chapters, Edwards looks at key issues like evangelism, interpreting the Bible, dealing with doubt, and surviving the church from the perspective of a confirmed, but sometimes reluctant, introvert. In the process, he offers some provocative insights that introverts will find helpful and reassuring.   *978-1-57312-681-6 144 pages/pb* **$15.00**

Reading Ezekiel (Reading the Old Testament series)
A Literary and Theological Commentary
Marvin A. Sweeney

The book of Ezekiel points to the return of YHWH to the holy temple at the center of a reconstituted Israel and creation at large. As such, the book of Ezekiel portrays the purging of Jerusalem, the Temple, and the people, to reconstitute them as part of a new creation at the conclusion of the book. With Jerusalem, the Temple, and the people so purged, YHWH stands once again in the holy center of the created world.

978-1-57312-658-8 264 pages/pb **$22.00**

Reading Hosea–Micah
(Reading the Old Testament series)
A Literary and Theological Commentary
Terence E. Fretheim

Terence E. Fretheim explores themes of indictment, judgment, and salvation in Hosea–Micah. The indictment against the people of God especially involves issues of idolatry, as well as abuse of the poor and needy. The effects of such behaviors are often horrendous in their severity. While God is often the subject of such judgments, the consequences, like fruit, grow out of the deed itself.   *978-1-57312-687-8 224 pages/pb* **$22.00**

Reading Samuel (Reading the Old Testament series)
A Literary and Theological Commentary

Johanna W. H. van Wijk-Bos

Interpreted masterfully by preeminent Old Testament scholar Johanna W. H. van Wijk-Bos, the story of Samuel touches on a vast array of subjects that make up the rich fabric of human life. The reader gains an inside look at leadership, royal intrigue, military campaigns, occult practices, and the significance of religious objects of veneration.

978-1-57312-607-6 272 pages/pb **$22.00**

Sessions with Genesis (Session Bible Studies series)
The Story Begins

Tony W. Cartledge

Immersing us in the book of Genesis, Tony W. Cartledge examines both its major stories and the smaller cycles of hope and failure, of promise and judgment. Genesis introduces these themes of divine faithfulness and human failure in unmistakable terms, tracing Israel's beginning to the creation of the world and professing a belief that Israel's particular history had universal significance.

978-1-57312-636-6 144 pages/pb **$14.00**

Sessions with Revelation (Session Bible Studies series)
The Final Days of Evil

David Sapp

David Sapp's careful guide through Revelation demonstrates that it is a letter of hope for believers; it is less about the last days of history than it is about the last days of evil. Without eliminating its mystery, Sapp unlocks Revelation's central truths so that its relevance becomes clear.

978-1-57312-706-6 166 pages/pb **$14.00**

Silver Linings
My Life Before and After *Challenger 7*

June Scobee Rodgers

We know the public story of *Challenger 7*'s tragic destruction. That day, June's life took a new direction that ultimately led to the creation of the Challenger Center and to new life and new love. Her story of Christian faith and triumph over adversity will inspire readers of every age.

978-1-57312-570-3 352 pages/hc **$28.00**

978-1-57312-694-6 352 pages/pb **$18.00**

Spacious
Exploring Faith and Place
Holly Sprink

Exploring where we are and why that matters to God is an ongoing process. If we are present and attentive, God creatively and continuously widens our view of the world. *978-1-57312-649-6 156 pages/pb* **$16.00**

The Teaching Church
Congregation as Mentor
Christopher M. Hamlin / Sarah Jackson Shelton

Collected in *The Teaching Church: Congregation as Mentor* are the stories of the pastors who shared how congregations have shaped, nurtured, and, sometimes, broken their resolve to be faithful servants of God. *978-1-57312-682-3 112 pages/pb* **$13.00**

A Time to Laugh
Humor in the Bible
Mark E. Biddle

An extension of his well-loved seminary course on humor in the Bible, *A Time to Laugh* draws on Mark E. Biddle's command of Hebrew language and cultural subtleties to explore the ways humor was intentionally incorporated into Scripture. With characteristic liveliness, Biddle guides the reader through the stories of six biblical characters who did rather unexpected things. *978-1-57312-683-0 164 pages/pb* **$14.00**

This Is What a Preacher Looks Like
Sermons by Baptist Women in Ministry
Pamela Durso, ed.

In this collection of sermons by thirty-six Baptist women, their voices are soft and loud, prophetic and pastoral, humorous and sincere. They are African American, Asian, Latina, and Caucasian. They are sisters, wives, mothers, grandmothers, aunts, and friends.

978-1-57312-554-3 144 pages/pb **$18.00**

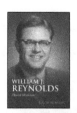

William J. Reynolds
Church Musician
David W. Music

William J. Reynolds is renowned among Baptist musicians, music ministers, song leaders, and hymnody students. In eminently readable style, David W. Music's comprehensive biography describes Reynolds's family and educational background, his career as a minister of music, denominational leader, and seminary professor. *978-1-57312-690-8 358 pages/pb* **$23.00**

9 781573 123266